'CALL ME HANK':
A STÓ:LŌ MAN'S REFLECTIONS ON LOGGING, LIVING, AND GROWING OLD

Henry Pennier

Edited by Keith Thor Carlson and Kristina Fagan

'My name is Henry George Pennier and if you want to be a friend of mine please you will call me Hank.' So begins 'Call Me Hank,' the autobiography of Hank Pennier (1904–1991): logger, storyteller, and self-described 'half breed.' In this work, Pennier offers thoughtful reflections on growing up as a non-status Aboriginal person on or near a Stó:lō reserve, searching for work of all kinds during hard times as a young man, and working as a logger through the depression of the 1930s up to his retirement. Known only to a small local audience when it was first published in 1972, this expanded edition of Pennier's autobiography provides poignant political commentary on issues of race, labour, and life through the eyes of a retired West Coast Native logger.

'Call Me Hank' is an engaging and often humorous read that makes an important contribution to a host of contemporary discourses in Canada, including discussions about the nature and value of Aboriginal identity. To Hank's original manuscript, Keith Carlson and Kristina Fagan have added a scholarly introduction situating Hank's writing within historical, literary, and cultural contexts, exploring his ideas and writing style, and offering further information about his life. A map of place names mentioned by Hank, a diagram of a steam logging operation, a glossary of logging terms, and sixteen photographs provide practical and historical complements to Pennier's original lively personal narrative.

Pennier's book preceded the proliferation of Aboriginal writing that began with the publication of Maria Campbell's *Halfbreed* in 1973 and provides a markedly different view of Aboriginal life from other writings of the period. It also documents important aspects of Aboriginal participation in the wage-labour economy that have been overlooked by historians, and offers a unique reflection on masculinity, government policy, and industrialization.

KEITH THOR CARLSON is an assistant professor in the Department of History at the University of Saskatchewan.

KRISTINA FAGAN is an assistant professor in the Department of English at the University of Saskatchewan.

Chiefly Indian

by HENRY PENNIER

The
Warm and Witty
Story of a
British Columbia
Half Breed Logger

edited by
Herbert L. McDonald

HENRY PENNIER

'Call Me Hank':
A Stó:lõ Man's Reflections
on Logging, Living, and
Growing Old

Second Edition

EDITED BY KEITH THOR CARLSON
AND KRISTINA FAGAN

UNIVERSITY OF TORONTO PRESS
Toronto Buffalo London

© University of Toronto Press Incorporated 2006
Toronto Buffalo London
Printed in Canada

Reprinted 2009

ISBN: 978-0-8020-9426-1 (paper)
ISBN: 978-0-8020-9161-1 (cloth)

Printed on acid-free paper

Library and Archives Canada Cataloguing in Publication

Pennier, Henry, 1904–1991
  Call me Hank : a Stó:lo man's reflections on logging, living and growing
old / Hank Pennier ; with a new introduction, explanatory notes,
glossary, and appendices by Keith Thor Carlson and Kristina Fagan. –
2nd ed.

First published under title: Chiefly Indian.
ISBN: 978-0-8020-9161-1 (bound)
ISBN: 978-0-8020-9426-1 (pbk.)

  1. Pennier, Henry, 1904–1991.   2. Métis – British Columbia –
Biography.   3. Stalo Indians – Biography.   4. Loggers – British
Columbia – Biography.   I. Pennier, Henry, 1904–1991. Chiefly
Indian.   II. Carlson, Keith Thor.   III. Fagan, Kristina Rose, 1973– .
IV. Title.

E78.B9P4 2006   971.1004'9794350092   c2006-903830-9

University of Toronto Press acknowledges the financial assistance to
its publishing program of the Canada Council for the Arts and the
Ontario Arts Council.

University of Toronto Press acknowledges the financial support for its
publishing activities of the Government of Canada through the Book
Publishing Industry Development Program (BPIDP).

To Hank's son Henry 'Jumbo' Pennier Jr (January 1930 – March 2006), who contributed greatly to the preparation of this second edition of his father's book, but who, sadly, passed away shortly before it was released.

Contents

Illustrations follow page 50

Foreword to 2006 Edition

My name's Henry Pennier Jr, but everyone calls me Jumbo. It's not that I'm a big fellow, but I guess I was a pretty big baby. When I was born the doctor told my mom and dad that I was a little Jumbo, and the name stuck.

Like my dad, I was a logger most of my life. I worked in the bush for over fifty years, starting when I was sixteen. That was the year my dad told me it was time I started earning my own keep and taking care of myself. So he brought me to a logging camp. Being independent was a big thing for my dad. He'd had to work hard to get by as a half-breed, and he knew his kids would have to work too. He wanted us to get ready for it early. You can see what I mean if you read this book.

Dad was away working a lot of the time when I was growing up, but that didn't stop him from being a great role model. He was a good logger, a wise logger. He was also captain of his soccer team and the only Native player on the Salmon Bellies lacrosse team. They called him 'Smoked Whiteman'! He was a language expert and a writer too. He spoke English, Halq'eméylem, Nlakapamux, Lillooet, and Chinook, and he even invented a way of writing the Stó:lõ Halq'eméylem language. He had quite a memory. Toward the end of his life Dad was really active with the Coqualeetza Elders group over in Chilliwack. It meant a lot to him to keep our Native traditions alive.

In writing this book back around 1970 my dad was being a real role model. Not many Native people were writing books back then. Dad used to write all the time. He only went to grade three at residential school, but he wrote a book. He was writing a second one, about the history of Natives, but he never had a chance to finish it. In this here book he tells you a lot about our Stó:lō community, our family, about old-style logging, and mostly about Dad. If you read it you'll learn a lot of things. I've read it four times myself and I find out something different every time. And you'll laugh too. Dad had a great sense of humour. He used to call me his number one son, like Charlie Chan, but I was his only son!

I remember when Dad's book first came out. He never talked about it that much, but he felt good, he was so happy. He'd head down to the Mission City Bingo and everyone had a copy of *Chiefly Indian*. He signed quite a few copies. I guess a few even found their way around the world. Dad got letters and postcards from people as far away as England and even Africa. Since Dad and I had the same name, some of the letters came to me by mistake. I remember when my wife saw the stamp she joked that I had a girlfriend in Africa. But this book isn't exactly the same as it was when Dad first published it. My friend Keith Carlson and Kristina Fagan have added a new section in the front, telling you more about Dad, along with pictures, a map, and some other stuff. So you'll get all of Dad's book, and then some. I hope you enjoy it.

Henry 'Jumbo' Pennier Jr
Chehalis, BC, 2006

Acknowledgments

We greatly appreciate the encouragement and help of Hank Pennier's friends and relatives who assisted us as we steered Hank's book through the publication of a second edition. We are especially grateful to Henry 'Jumbo' Pennier Jr, Patricia Kelly, Laura Kelly, Clarence 'Kat' Pennier, Mabel (Lawrence) Nichols, Alan Gutierrez, and Albert 'Sonny' McHalsie. Inez Point was a great help in identifying appropriate photographs at the Chilliwack Museum and Archives, as was MacKinley Darlington, who also helped with copy editing. We recognize and greatly appreciate the generosity of the Chilliwack Museum and Archives, especially Ron Denman and Kelly Harms, for allowing us to reproduce historical photographs from their collections. We are also grateful to Jan Perrier for designing the map and diagram found in this edition. Additionally, we acknowledge the helpful comments provided on earlier versions of this expanded manuscript by J.R. Miller, John Porter, M.T. Carlson, Sonny McHalsie, David Smith, Jill McConkey, and the two anonymous reviewers with the University of Toronto Press. And of course we are deeply indebted to Wyn Roberts for having taken the steps that sparked Hank to put pen to paper, and finally and most deeply to Hank Pennier himself for having taken the time to share his thoughts and reflections.

Introduction to 2006 Edition

Henry Pennier was not the sort of person who attracted a lot of attention during the first sixty-five years of his life – especially from 'white people.' So, family members recall him being a little surprised when, in 1969, Wyn Roberts, a young linguist from Simon Fraser University, travelled ninety kilometres east of Vancouver on Highway 7 to interview Pennier about the Halq'eméylem language and related Stó:lō Aboriginal traditions. As a 'half-breed' who had spent his years negotiating an identity in the 'no man's land' of Canadian racial politics, Pennier found a certain irony in being identified by an academic as a valued expert on Aboriginal traditions. In the foreword to the original 1972 edition of this volume, Roberts explains that he had very particular goals in making this trip: he wanted to test some linguistic theories that he was developing. He also hoped that he could collect some 'old Indian stories of ... legendary, god-like figures' (xli). But Henry Pennier had ideas of his own.

Roberts asked Pennier (who quickly made it plain that he preferred to be called Hank) to think of Halq'eméylem words and 'Indian stories,' and told him that he would come back in a week to record them on audiotape. When he returned the following Sunday, he found that Hank had written out his story – not a 'legend' but a humorous anecdote he had heard in his youth, and he had written it in English. Over the next few months, Hank continued to write, producing a series of anecdotal reminiscences. He eventually published this collection of autobiographical writings, with editorial assistance from his friend Roberts and local Vancouver author/publisher Herb McDonald, under the title *Chiefly Indian: The Warm and Witty Story of a British Columbia Half Breed Logger*. That work is reproduced here under the new title *'Call Me Hank': A Stó:lō Man's Reflections on Logging, Living, and Growing Old*. Other than the new title, Hank's writing appears here almost exactly as it did in the 1972 edition. His original manuscript has been lost, and there are no records of the changes Mac-Donald made to the text when he 'assembled and smoothed lightly the stories into a chronological whole' (xliv), so the 1972 edition is the only available version. We have standardized the spelling, with the exception of any spelling that reflects a distinctive pronunciation (i.e., 'shure,' 'likkered,' 'berthing'). We have also added apostrophes where they were occasionally missing and corrected a few errors that were obviously typographical. The small errors and idiosyncrasies in the 1972 edition may have been introduced by Hank, Roberts, or the printer, and we felt that Hank would have wanted his book to appear in the most polished form possible. Similar concerns motivated our title change. We do not know who conceived the original title, and while we like the play on the word 'Chiefly' in as much as it refers to Hank's having been 'principally' or 'primarily' Aboriginal, the second meaning, in our opinion, was not in keeping with the unassuming way Hank Pennier thought of himself and presented himself. In addition to these changes and the composition of this introductory essay, we have added explanatory endnotes, a glossary of logging terms, and a number of photos and illustrations to help readers become more fully engaged in Hank's world. And finally, we have appended a brief biographical sketch of Hank's grandfather George Perrier, and a transcript of a 1972 interview in which Hank proudly discusses his recently printed book while providing his listeners with somewhat different renditions of a few of the stories contained in that volume.

Like the young Professor Roberts, many non-Aboriginal people think that they know, even before they have listened, what Aboriginal people will say. They assume that there is an 'Aboriginal perspective.' Hank Pennier's autobiography, however, reminds us that there is no single or simple Aboriginal voice. Wading fearlessly into issues of race, culture, identity, masculinity, politics, labour, technology, and aging, Hank writes from his own unique perspective and experience. Being part of the Stó:lō community while working in the white-dominated logging industry, Hank had the chance to look at the world from many angles. When, in 1959, four decades of cumulative workplace injuries forced him to exit the logging industry prematurely, time that had formerly been occupied with labour became filled with bitter-sweet reminiscences, humorous reflections, and contemplation. What Hank Pennier chose to say in his autobiography does not fit neatly into any school of thought and will surprise, trouble, and delight people of all political persuasions.

Hank's initial decision not to write what Roberts had asked of him tells us a great deal about this strong-willed man. Of course, more than thirty years after the fact, and fifteen years since his death on 8 October 1991, we cannot know for certain why Hank initially decided not to relate for Roberts the kind of Aboriginal legends for which the aspiring young academic was hoping. It is not that he was incapable of fulfilling the request. Hank was fluent in Halq'eméylem; indeed, he had devised his own practical orthography so he could write it with English letters and not lose the Aboriginal pronunciation. Furthermore, contemporary Stó:lō elders remember Hank Pennier as having been a cultural expert. Perhaps, when Roberts first approached him, Hank felt a reluctance to pass certain sacred stories to a broader audience through someone he had only just met: once out of his control, they might be misunderstood or misused. Perhaps despite his considerable reputation, initially he felt unqualified to communicate such stories and to speak as an authority with a scholar on certain aspects of tradition. Humility and caution are highly valued traits among the Stó:lō. Showing such humility, early in part 1 Hank observes that if he had been 'smarter' he would have 'listened a lot harder and learned a lot more' from his stepfather's father, Billy Swallsea, who regularly shared traditional stories with him as he was growing up (7). Ultimately Hank did decide to include some traditional stories in the published version of his writings, but he never depicts himself as a cultural expert.

There is no doubt that Hank was well-versed in Stó:lō traditions, but in his writings he refused to be identified only as a voice of tradition. Just as Hank had asserted his right to be called by the name he chose, he took control of which stories he would tell and how they would be presented to the world. In doing so, he challenged popular stereotypes of 'Indians' and 'half-breeds' as well as federal categorizations of Aboriginal people. And he shaped a very complex self-portrait. Over the course of his recollections, Hank identifies himself in a variety of ways – as a 'half breed' (5), an 'Indian' (52), and 'just good old Hank' (86) – and his judgments of these labels also vary. For Hank Pennier, as for all of us, identity operated differently in different situations and in different relationships.

At the beginning of his story, Hank identifies himself as 'what the white man calls a half breed, and why not since I have been one all my life' (5). But being a half-breed did not mean that one of Hank's parents was Indian and the other white, nor was it a reference to living within what in the Canadian prairies would have been called a Metis community. In British Columbia, 'half-breed' was a pejorative title attached to anyone of Native ancestry who did not have Indian status but who looked like and lived like an

Aboriginal person. It was a negative designation that reflected the racial and gender prejudices of mainstream Canadian society.

Hank admits that he knew very little about the man who had introduced the Pennier name into the Stó:lō community – not even his first name. He writes that he remembers having been told that his paternal grandfather came to the Fraser Valley from Quebec and there met and married Hank's grandmother and sired his father. Hank also knew that his grandfather had been murdered while on a trip back east when his son (Hank's father) was only a young child. Archival research reveals that Hank's grandfather's name was actually George John Perrier, a sailor with the Hudson's Bay Company (HBC) who went on to play a brief, if rather controversial, role in British Columbia's early colonial history during the 1858 Fraser River gold rush (see appendix 1).

Subsequent to his colourful government service, George Perrier built and ran the Colonial Hotel at Yale. Then, after the enthusiasm for mining waned, he homesteaded on the fertile lands near the junction of the Harrison and Chehalis Rivers in the central Fraser Valley (see map). It is there, presumably, that he met and married Suzanne Chiltlat, of the adjacent Stó:lō settlement of Chehalis.[1] Their son George Jr was born at Chehalis in 1869. After George senior's death (ca. 1875), Suzanne and her son returned to her Stó:lō community on the Harrison River. There being no equivalent for the English 'r' sound in the Stó:lō people's Halq'eméylem language, the young George Perrier II came to be known officially as George Pennier.[2] In 1889 'Pennier' married Alice Davis (whose father, William Davis, was an American citizen who had been born, and later returned and died, in Wales). Alice Davis's mother, Daelali Rosalie Siamelouet, was from a high-status Stó:lō family on the Lakahaman reserve near Mission City. Together George and Alice had eight children. Henry 'Hank' George Pennier, the youngest, was born in February 1904, three months after the untimely death of his father, George. The widow Alice and her four surviving children then relocated to the Indian reserve known as Union Bar, near Hope, where she had been born thirty-five years earlier. There she became acquainted with Chief August Billy, a widower with eight children of his own, and in 1910 the two were married in the local Catholic church. August Billy also came from a prominent Stó:lō family. His father, Billy Swallsea (who spent a great deal of time teaching his young step-grandson Hank Pennier about Stó:lō culture and traditions), carried the hereditary name of the original ancestor of the lower Fraser Canyon Ts'ó:kw'em tribe.[3] The name Swallsea was also associated with the origin of the sacred Sxwó:yxwey mask.[4] When Hank turned twenty he married Margaret Leon from Chehalis, and together they had six children.[5]

In Hank's words, he and Margaret and all their children were 'half breeds. Not white men and not Indian yet we look Indian and every body but Indians takes us for Indian. It's been a complicated world ... And the government hasn't helped any' (6). Here he points out the problems of public perception and government categorization that made it a 'complicated world' for him and his family. His identity as a half-breed was largely imposed upon him by non-Native society. Though Hank Pennier had more Aboriginal than European blood flowing through his veins, and despite the fact that he had been raised by Stó:lō people in a Stó:lō environment where rights, status, and names were traditionally transmitted bilaterally (that is, through both the mother's and the father's line), he was non-Native as far as the Canadian government was concerned. This categorization was based in the sexism of Canadian Indian policy as it applied to Aboriginal identity. Hank's grandmother Suzanne lost her Indian status when she married the Québécois George Perrier. Their son George, therefore, never had Indian status, and so neither did Hank (although he was technically entitled to it after being adopted by Chief Billy). Hank's wife Margaret also lost her status upon marrying Hank, and so all of Hank's descendants were ineligible for status until the government amended the Indian Act with Bill C-31 in 1985. As a result, although he sometimes 'felt all Indian' (21), Hank was not legally permitted to live on an Indian reserve and had 'no [Indian] agency to look after [him]' (86).

This position had its advantages and disadvantages. Hank Pennier was technically a Canadian citizen, with all the rights and privileges that this implied. He could legally vote in federal and provincial elections, own property, and purchase and consume liquor while his status Indian friends and relatives could not. And yet the colour of his skin prevented him from enjoying many of the privileges that Canadian citizenship supposedly conferred. Being a half-breed in the first half of the twentieth century meant confronting disadvantage without institutional or community support. 'Outside of my work,' he writes, 'I could not join the white society, socially' (87). With bitter humour he explains that he was not welcome at white people's parties, but if he was caught at a party where status Indians were drinking, he risked being arrested because people assumed he, too, was a status Indian – and under Canadian law various prohibitions restricted Native people's (and occasionally newcomers') ability to legally purchase, sell, or consume alcohol. On one occasion Hank was fined $300 for having giving a ride to Native friends who had been drinking, and on another he was arrested and charged an additional $300 for 'supplying' – that is to say, the police arrived at his house and found that he had given a bottle of beer to a visiting Aboriginal friend. Allegedly to recoup the money the legal system had cost him, Hank tried his hand at bootlegging for a while, but was caught and had to pay yet another $300 fine. Indeed, such was the hypocrisy of Canadian law and the zealousness of Canadian police that Hank claims he was even charged with what he terms 'kniving,' simply for having an Aboriginal person in his car as well as a sealed bottle of whisky. The crime? As Hank saw it, 'the intention of giving [an Indian] a drink sooner or later' (87).

Despite having been labelled a half-breed by white society, Hank appears to have been considered Stó:lō by his Aboriginal friends and family. His stepfather and step-grandfather were particularly traditional men (a point that Hank is careful to note more than once), and it was through them and his mother that Hank acquired much of his cultural knowledge. More than a decade after the publication of *Chiefly Indian*, as Hank neared the end of his life, he was widely acknowledged as a respected member of the Coqualeetza Elders group – a community of Stó:lō elders who, to this day, meet weekly at the site of the old Coqualeetza Residential School and Indian Tuberculosis Hospital in Chilliwack, BC, to share their cultural traditions and promote the Halq'eméylem language.[6] Moreover, Hank carried the hereditary names of Cinda and Swegh-tin. To the end, Hank valued being Aboriginal and preserving Aboriginal culture, but he never thought highly of being 'Indian' as defined by the Indian Act.

Hank was also aware that, despite the Indian Act label, he was subject to the same stereotypes as his friends with status. Throughout his writing, he plays with and against the expectations of his largely non-Aboriginal audience. At one point, for example, after telling the story of a flood that cut off the electricity to his home, Hank acknowledges that his audience might have been surprised to learn that an Aboriginal family like his would find it difficult to get by without electrical appliances: 'I suppose you think that is funny since I am Indian sort of' (52). Here, as in other places, Hank anticipates that his audience's impressions of him would likely be shaped by stereotypes. Thus, perhaps in an attempt to educate his audience, he often comments on issues of racism and stereotyping that he faced at work (50) and in the world at large: 'I like good shootup detective movies and western movies the best but in the westerns with all those Indians which always get the worst of things and always get shot up, I can't put any faith. It's all pretty phoney because Indians were a lot smarter than that and still are for that matter' (75–6).

The stereotype that seems to bother Hank most was the way that Indians had been typecast as 'lazy,' and he clearly wants to prove to his audience that he does not fit that mould. Deflecting stereotypes associated with 'lazy Indians' became particularly important for Hank after work-related injuries compelled him to leave the workforce prematurely in 1959 and placed him in the position of depending on welfare:

> I see all this talk on TV the past couple of years about all the Indians on welfare and I think by golly, that's me they are talking about too. Think Hank I say to myself. Maybe you earned the right better than some others I say, and if it wasn't for all those accidents you had could be you would still be working and pulling your weight ... It was thoughts like this that drove me near crazy the first five or six years after I [stopped working]. (76)

It was not that he did not want to be Native, or to be associated with Native society; he just did not want to be associated with what non-Native society so often – and pejoratively – associated with 'Indianness': 'Way back in the woods among the trees doing a man's work, I wasn't a half breed, I was just good old Hank' (86).

Pondering the issues of racism and governmental injustices that he had experienced, as well as the suffering he anticipated for his young grandchildren and foster children, Hank Pennier wonders in his autobiography what pragmatic solutions there might be. He was writing in the late 1960s and early 1970s, just as Pierre Trudeau's government was proposing to eliminate Indian status, and when British Columbia Aboriginal people had no meaningful role in the management of the resources of their territory.

From his vantage point, he could not have foreseen such important judicial decisions as the *Sparrow, Guerin,* and *Delgamuukw* cases, which gave legal status and protection to a variety of Aboriginal rights, or the related political developments that led to the establishment of the BC treaty process – developments that significantly strengthened the hand of indigenous people vis à vis mainstream Canadian society. Given the social context of the times, it is not surprising that Hank determines that the best solution is to eliminate issues of official status altogether. In the conclusion to this volume he asserts, with some frustration, 'Why shouldn't there be just people now? No Indians. No Eskimos. No whites. Just people. Maybe some day it will be like that but I know I won't be around then. Too bad because there won't be any half breeds either and that will be a damn good thing' (86).

Such sentiments appear to contradict the opposition Aboriginal leaders across Canada mounted against Trudeau's 1969 proposal to integrate Aboriginal people into the Canadian body politic as citizens like any other ethnic group. Indeed, a decade after the publication of *Chiefly Indian,* and still a decade before the creation of the BC Treaty Commission, Hank counselled his non-status relatives not to take advantage of the 1985 amendments to the Indian Act (known as Bill C-31) that entitled them to regain Indian status – advice they largely rejected. But to categorize Hank Pennier as a supporter of Trudeau's vision, or as an opponent of indigenous rights, would be to miss the nuance of his personal philosophy and the depth of his commitment to preserving Aboriginal culture and traditions.

Hank both despised and came to value his identification as a half-breed. It was a designation, Hank asserted, that presented a challenge greater than that faced by either status Indians or non-Native Canadian citizens. Caught in the middle, Hank took the cards fate had dealt him and turned what was ostensibly a 'nothing hand' into a 'full house.' As a half-breed, he determined that he needed to create opportunities out of deficits. His only avenue for accomplishing this was through hard work, determination, and a driving ambition to show that he was more, and better, than people would at first give him credit for. If society regarded a half-breed as inferior to both a full-status Indian and a non-Native white, Hank demonstrated that the term could also refer to someone who was more than the sum of either of his ethnic identities: 'What I think the real trouble today is nobody has any ambition anymore to be a better work man than the next guy or to turn out a first class piece of work. I guess those days are over and its just too damn bad I think. I also think they should a been born half breeds then they would know how to work hard to make their way and stay ahead and be better than another guy' (54).

As this passage shows, it was through the dignity of labour that Hank found a way to be respected in this 'complicated world.' Through hard physical labour in the logging industry, Hank achieved status within mainstream society's definition of masculinity, a society that devalued Aboriginal people and made no space for people of mixed ancestry. Hard work enabled him to feel as good as, or better than, other men. It was after a hard day's work, he says, that 'a man can feel like he's standing ten feet tall' (61). While the 1930s is generally considered to have been a sad and disempowering time for Canadians, and especially for indigenous people, for Hank Pennier the Great Depression was a remarkable decade. It was during the thirties that his personal philosophy stressing the value of hard work and ambition was solidified and validated, for it was then, in the midst of international economic chaos, that the social and racial orders were temporarily inverted. The 1929 stock market crash created an extremely tight and competitive job market. Coastal logging companies, Hank Pennier's principal employers, were compelled to streamline. Hard workers, therefore, were valued, and by this standard Hank had clearly demonstrated his worth.

Within months of the 1929 Black Monday crash, when many men were suddenly struggling with unemployment, Hank Pennier found himself solicited to hire his own crew of similarly minded and skilled individuals, regardless of the men's race. As he proudly notes, throughout the Depression he was never without work, and indeed his income and status rose significantly. Hank traded in the currency of masculine hard work to balance the weight of racial prejudice. His experiences, however, should not necessarily be regarded as typical. Many Aboriginal people found themselves disadvantaged throughout the 1930s, and efforts to start or sustain band-based Native logging companies faced special challenges. Racism became even more pronounced in many labour fields.[7] Nonetheless, as a result of the general economic downturn, employment advantages that had previously flowed exclusively to other people because of their skin colour and education were occasionally neutralized, and Hank was quick to seize the chance. On one occasion, he even found himself supervising two otherwise unemployable white university professors as they performed the mundane task of checking railcar wheels for cracks (49). Logging, as it was practised prior to the Second World War, was no place for soft intellectuals. It was, in Hank's words, 'man's work and risky. This last reason is the best one I think because it means an Indian can feel as good as the next guy and from what we see of a lot of whites these days, maybe even better than the next guy. So with me as a half breed which is neither one or the other, that reason is I guess the best of all' (58).

Logging was also work that Hank regarded as consistent with his Stó:lō traditions. As is common among indigenous people, the Stó:lō consider humans to be a part of nature, not above it, as was long a tenet of Western Christian philosophy.[8] In this world view, people are entitled to use and benefit from plants and animals, but such use is informed by a desire to create and sustain balance and harmony. Indeed, power and status come from succeeding in balanced situations. Victory that is predetermined by a technology that creates an unfair advantage for humans over plants or animals (or even other human adversaries) is often regarded by the Stó:lō as hollow and vapid. For that reason, some Stó:lō men engaged in activities that outsiders regarded as excessively difficult, dangerous, and even foolhardy. Rather than using spears, deadfall traps, or rifles to hunt grizzly bears, for example, certain Stó:lō men chose as their weapon only a 24 cm sharpened bone. Such hunters approached the bears directly and waited for the attack. They knew that at close quarters, as bears lunge forward, the great beasts inevitably open their mouths. It was at this point, with the bear descending upon him, that the Stó:lō hunter thrust the sharpened bone into the bear's mouth, causing the point to pierce the roof of the mouth and puncture the brain, killing the animal almost instantly. There were easier and safer ways to dispose of a grizzly, but none that brought such acclaim or status, for in killing the bear when the odds were at least as favourable for the grizzly as the hunter, a man demonstrated much more about his character than an easy victory with a rifle or a deadfall ever could. What is more, he acquired potent spirit power from his defeated adversary.[9]

While Hank discusses grizzly hunting only twice in his prose, both anecdotes are significant. In one, Hank describes hunting bear with a rifle, but the thrill of the kill was profound: 'I sure felt all Indian that day,' he tells us (21). The bear kill provided him with a sense of racial balance that too often was lacking in his life as constructed by outsiders. The second bear anecdote, discussed later in this introduction, also depicts bear hunting as a source of personal fulfillment and balance (see xxvii–xxviii). Similarly, his discussion of his efforts to achieve victory through balanced and harmonious competition with giant Douglas firs are clearly informed by the same epistemological assumptions. Steam logging and handsaws made Hank feel 'big' in a world of giant trees. They empowered him, but not to the point of overpowering nature. He respected the towering firs because he knew that they had a fair chance against him: 'In my time it took two men at each end of a ten foot crosscut saw bucking away for most of a day before old Mr. Fir would give up the ghost. We always knew who was going to win but at least we gave him the chance of putting up a fight for it. And some times in spite he would flip his butt as he died and take a man with him' (60). Men took trees, and sometimes trees took men. There was balance in Hank's world and occupation.

Born in the early years of the twentieth century, Hank witnessed and reluctantly participated in the rapid industrialization of the West Coast logging industry. The new technology that entered the industry after the Second World War ushered in changes that Hank saw as disrupting the sensitive balance between loggers and trees: 'I bet that the men who sit in those nice warm glassed-in cabs and move all those pedals and levers and throttles need engineers papers from some university to run them ... Where's the chance for a guy to get in there into the jungle with just his muscle and his brains and slug it out with a tough opponent?' (59). Hank explains that in his day 'things were different.' 'You take a virgin Douglas Fir tree that has spent maybe two hundred, three hundred years to grow straight and maybe two hundred feet high and that is about eight feet through at the butt. In my thinking which I know is old fashioned I think there is some thing dirty about a man now who is able to cut it crashing down in less than half a hour all by himself using a six foot gasoline chain saw. What chance does the poor tree have?' (59–60).

Hank Pennier was not alone, of course, in regarding the trees of the forest as capable and worthy opponents. Many of his 'old-timer' non-Native friends undoubtedly anthropomorphised trees and occasionally equipment in much the same way. What set Hank apart was his indigenous belief that all things – even manufactured inanimate objects – are genuinely sentient. In the Stó:lō world view, life force (*shxweli*) inhabits all things, including trees and rocks, and residual spirit power from humans and their spirit helpers inform and help animate objects such as dip nets, arrows, and spears. With the arrival of European new-comers this belief was extended to include introduced objects as well. That is to say, new things were incorporated into the Stó:lō world view at least as much as, if not more than, the Stó:lō world view was altered by new things. A commonly shared story within contemporary Stó:lō com-munities tells of a spirit dancer from Sumas whose spirit helper came from a steam locomotive. Perhaps it is within this vein that Hank's wonderful account of Chief Johnny, who fell asleep with his feet too close to a woodstove and awoke to find the soles of his boots scorched, is best appre-ciated: 'He bawled out the stove for five minutes and after that the old stove never did keep him quite so warm again' (53). That anecdote, told to Hank when he was just a child, reinforced his world view about the spirit energy in all things. 'I always remember that story when Temptation makes me want to swear at some piece of equipment that don't do what its supposed to do. Poor innocent stove' (53).

Throughout his autobiography, Hank Pennier seeks to challenge limitations in our perceptions, whether of trees, of Aboriginal people, or of himself. Indeed, this challenge was at the centre of the very first story he chose to write for Wyn Roberts. That first story described a 'great Indian bear hunter' who, at the age of ninety-eight, wanted to hunt a grizzly one last time. The hunter's two grandsons carried him on a stretcher back into the hills but, as soon as a bear appeared, the terrified boys dropped the stretcher and ran away. They arrived home crying about their grandfather's certain death. And, Hank concludes, 'the mother says to the boys stop crying you two, your grandpa got home a half

hour ago. Boy he sure must have been a tough old guy'
(44).

At the time that he wrote this story, Hank was sixty-five
years old and, as a result of injuries sustained while logging, scarcely able to walk. His immobility clearly bothered
him; he mused about needing to depend on welfare and
worker's compensation: 'How do I feel about that? Me
who was always independent and worked hard as I could
for what I earned? And was never without work for 39
years. Not very good but what else can I do about it now?'
(76). It was clearly not random selection that led Hank to
write the story of an old man who longs for the work that
once gave his life a sense of value. The story of the old
bear hunter who turns out to be faster than his grandsons
clearly appealed enormously to Hank. But more than that,
the story tells of an old man whose abilities go far beyond
what the young expect of him. Thus, the story of the great
bear hunter may have been a message to the young linguist, Wyn Roberts, and to other future readers, that Hank
Pennier was capable of more than they might at first
assume. Like the classic West Coast Aboriginal 'Trickster'
figure, Hank liked to use humour to show that things were
not always as they seemed, especially when it came to
Native–newcomer relations – a theme M. Holden subse-
quently documented as typical of Coast Salish oral narratives.[10] Though Hank's story of the great bear hunter now
appears in the middle of the book, this first story established the themes of individual choice and unexpected
ability in the face of limited expectations that run
throughout the many stories and recollections that Hank
went on to write.

The 'great bear hunter' anecdote reminds us of how
carefully Hank selected the stories that he would pen. It is
common, in reading Aboriginal autobiographies, for critics
to accept the work as a transparent recording of the teller's
'truth.' We can see a degree of this critical response in the
young Wyn Roberts's emphasis on the 'honesty and lack of

pretension' (xliii) in Hank's writing: 'Any way you look at it,' Roberts concludes, 'this book *is* Henry Pennier' (xliv). The appeal of such an approach to interpreting Aboriginal autobiography is obvious. The voice in Hank's writing – direct, casual, conversational – gives the impression that we can see directly into his life. But this is an illusion: this book *is not* Henry Pennier but, rather, it is something that he created, shaping and selecting events, emphasizing or repeating some things and leaving out others, carefully creating a portrait of himself for a principally non-Aboriginal audience. Hank Pennier was not only a logger, he was also a writer.

As a writer, Hank's primary form was the anecdote. A brief, often humorous, story, the anecdote is considered a traditionally oral genre. Hank likely refined and ultimately perfected the form while sitting with his fellow workers in camp after a day of logging. It is in such situations that one memory brings up another and the stories flow. The transcript of an interview with Hank Pennier that appears at the end of this edition reveals Hank as a master teller of anecdotes – setting the stage, building the tension, and then carefully timing the unexpected punchline. Within the book, Hank's narrative may appear to move from one such anecdote to another in a kind of free association. However, his selection of stories is not as random as it might first seem. He carefully chose and shaped them to create a particular impression. In the appended interview, for instance, he explains that he changed the setting of his story about giving the priest salt for his tea. While he tells his interviewers that the incident happened at his mother's house in Union Bar, in the book it takes place at residential school. Perhaps he felt that, within the context of the book, the story would fit well into a series of humorous stories about priests and church. He unapologetically explains that this creative revising of the past is a necessary part of writing: 'You know it's little different in my book, you know, you gotta change.'[11] Indeed, the style of this oral story is also significantly different from the version that appears in his book. Talking to his Stó:lō friends and relatives during the group interview, he salted the story with swear words as well as with references to local people and places that are lost on the outside reader. He clearly recognized that such a casual and familiar style might not be appropriate within his book. He never does explicitly explain why he changed the story, but in Stó:lō society aspects of personal reminiscences are occasionally altered for different audiences to disengage social tension or to enhance humour.[12] To those at the group interview, this was a story about Father Chirouse, a specific man in a specific place. For the primarily white audience of Hank's book, this was a story about a non-specific priest, and perhaps the details of place are less important than the theme of Hank's playfully challenging relationship to authority figures. Hank also freely admits that some stories have been left out altogether because they would not create the desired effect. In the final chapter he reflects openly about this exclusion, contemplating his own motivations for what he included and what he omitted in the preceding chapters: 'I think of being a altar boy, and my grandfather's stories, and the days in the woods with the big trees, and some of the girls that I used to know but I never told you about those did I? because I am a gentleman' (77). 'So I guess that's my story up to now or as much as I can remember of it and if I wanted to tell you the truth, as much as I want my wife to know about me. A man has to have some secrets' (88–9).

In fact, one of Hank's biggest 'secrets' in his book seems to be his relationships with his wife Margaret and their children. They are scarcely mentioned. His wedding is summed up briefly: 'When I was 20, I signed the lifelong contract for better or for worse. Which meant I really had to work for the rest of my life' (30). The lack of details and his wry tone when he mentions his wife, however, certainly do not mean that Hank's family was not important to him. For one, his identity as father and husband may not have fit into the image of masculinity and independence that he created for his readers. Another possibility is that not writing about his family members was, in fact, a sign of respect for them. While telling his own story, Hank pointedly excludes the personal stories of others, allowing them to maintain their privacy. This sense of privacy is seen in many Aboriginal autobiographies. For instance, Maria Campbell's *Halfbreed,* while revealing deeply personal incidents from her life, such as her struggles with prostitution and drug addiction, scarcely mentions her children. Similarly, while Cherokee writer Thomas King spoke revealingly about himself during his Massey lecture series, he did not mention his wife or children, and he could not bring himself to tell the story of his friends John and Amy Cardinal and their family problems. Though he does write about these friends in the book based on the lectures, he seems disturbed by his decision, explaining, 'The story about John and Amy Cardinal is not a story I want to tell. It is, quite probably, a story that I should not tell. It is certainly not a story that I would want anyone to hear.' The only reason King can bring himself to write about them is, he says, because this story is exclusively written rather than spoken out loud in a lecture theatre and it is therefore a 'private story'; oral stories, on the other hand, he says, are 'public stories.'[13] Indeed, Aboriginal oral traditions are often accompanied by beliefs that saying the wrong things can have serious consequences. Stó:lō traditions, for instance, warn that mistelling a story in the presence of a pregnant woman may cause her baby to be born with missing or extra limbs. Perhaps Hank Pennier, raised in this tradition of oral and public stories, was particularly careful in whom he spoke about and how he spoke about them.

Hank's humorous spirit may also have been learned in his Stó:lō community. Salish people have a strong tradition of witty, satirical, and ironic stories that challenge authority, whether that be the authority of 'the whiteman,' or of traditional Salish culture.[14] Many of Hank's stories were in this line. He clearly enjoyed relating anecdotes that displayed cleverness and strength in the face of low public expectations – especially if they included humorous twists reminiscent of the classic Native Trickster stories. Side by side in his repertoire are accounts of a Stó:lō boy whose entire family was massacred by Lekwiltok raiders from the coast near Campbell River but who nonetheless grew up to be a powerful Indian doctor, and the story of 'Ollie the logger' who registered in a hotel as Dr Ollie and ended up being called upon to deliver a baby – which he did with ease. Whether they were his own or those of other similarly disadvantaged people, Hank Pennier revelled in unanticipated accomplishments. He was just enough of a rogue to enjoy challenging and occasionally taking advantage of the system and assumptions that had disadvantaged him. Yet, in keeping with Aboriginal storytelling traditions, he rarely explains the 'moral' of these humorous stories, allowing readers to interpret them on their own. Vi Hilbert, a Puget Sound Salish historian, remembers her own childhood experience of listening to humorous stories from her elders: 'While the stories were told to me in great detail, allowing for my delicate ears, the moral was never, ever explained to me.'[15] Hank's stories are a way for him to teach the attitudes and values that allowed him to achieve a sense of success and self-worth. But just as importantly, his sense of humour seems to help him to deal with troubles and injustices. For instance, after working in the logging industry all his life, Hank finished his career filling potholes – a job that clearly humiliated him. Yet he quips. 'Funny thing was if you remember, my first job in 1920 was wheeling sawdust at a mill, where I used a big scoop shovel, and I ended 39 years later on the end of another kind of shovel' (73). Lakota scholar Vine Deloria writes that such a sense of humour has allowed Aboriginal people to survive colonization: 'When a people can laugh at themselves and laugh at others and hold all aspects of life together without letting anyone drive them to extremes, then it would seem to me that the people can survive.'[16] Hank Pennier was undoubtedly a survivor – and a celebrator – of life, even in the worst of times.

For Hank, the worst of times seems to have been the period of his life after his injuries forced him to retire at the age of fifty-five. Deprived of the work that had been such an important part of his identity, the limitations of age and disability grated: 'I am not an old man yet by a damn sight, although with only the little bit I can get around I sure as hell act like one' (75). The final chapter of the book, which describes this period of Hank's life, reflects on a world that, for him, had become physically smaller, a world focused on his home, his television, and his bingo games. Yet while his frustration is evident, Hank finds relief in his thoughts, memories, and dreams: 'Best time for me these days is when I am sleeping. That's when I can lead a double life' (84). Waking hours were pensive and often more difficult. 'I just go on from day to day living from day to day and I watch the seasons pass across my window ... and I think about being an alter boy, and my grand father's stories, and the days in the woods in the big trees, and some of the girls I used to know' (77). He even composes dramatic narratives about the animals he sees outside his window. And, of course, this was the period of his life when Hank began to write, an activity that he says 'makes the days pass easier' (89), thus once again turning limitations into opportunity. Perhaps it was this creative work that allowed Hank to move towards acceptance of his body's restrictions: 'I found that it takes a man one hell of a long time to accept the fates but that no matter how hard you fight it there comes a time when you just learn to accept it all and stop fighting' (77), though he suddenly interrupts his philosophizing to joke: 'Hey Hank that's enough about that. You sound like an old man which I am certainly not' (77).

Overall, Hank's depiction of old age is unexpectedly optimistic. Readers may also be surprised to read his relatively positive and sympathetic portrayal of Catholic Church officials and of St Mary's Residential School. As a 'half-breed,' Hank was technically not entitled to attend a federally funded Indian school, but, he recalls, in his case, 'the priests were kind and made an exception' (9). It might be tempting to ascribe Hank's perspective to the era in which he was writing. The systemic physical and sexual abuse that we now know characterized so many residential school students' experiences had not been fully and publicly exposed. Yet even without this added sinister context, such influential and widely publicized studies as H.B. Hawthorn's 1967 *Survey of the Contemporary Indians of Canada* had already condemned residential schools for creating an environment where students 'come to value themselves less and to strive to do less as they get no benefit; they are confused as to what they should be and do; they do not live in a setting where schools prove themselves either happy or useful; [and] they withdraw when they can, psychologically or bodily.'[17] But if such was a part of Hank's experiences, he chose not to communicate it in print. In this regard, what he remembered and decided to share is similar to some of the more recent public expressions related by some former students of the Catholic and Methodist residential schools operating in Stó:lō territory.[18] And so here again, as in so many others instances, Hank invites us to view the world through a lens that is different from the one we anticipate. For him, apparently, residential school provided a relatively fun and safe environment, and it was only 'after [he] got out [that] things were never quite so nice again' (13).

Given the richness, range, and uniqueness of his writing, it is unfortunate that literary scholars and historians alike have largely overlooked Hank Pennier. Hank is not the only Aboriginal writer from BC whom the public has largely forgotten. Alan Twigg documents many others in *Aboriginality: The Literary Origins of British Columbia*. It seems that Indians writing colourful, humorous, and generally happy anecdotes were not what readers were looking for in the early 1970s. One reviewer at the time expressed 'disappointment' that Hank had presented neither the magical appeal of 'a mythical logger' nor the activist anger of 'an articulate half-Indian writing about the dynamics of race prejudice in the logging industry.' Instead, what the reviewer claims to have found was a 'series of single framed shots, ... the kind of thoughts that come along when the body's busy but the mind rolls on.'[19]

Others seem to have shared these views, for the current wealth of Aboriginal writing in Canada is widely considered to have been kick-started by Campbell's 1973 autobiography, *Halfbreed*, which appeared the year after Hank's *Chiefly Indian*. After Campbell, the next-most-cited text in this genre is Beatrice Culleton's 1983 fictionalized autobiography, *In Search of April Raintree*, and similar to both are the works of Lee Maracle, a woman of mixed Stó:lō and Cree ancestry who in 1975 published *Bobbi Lee, Indian Rebel: Struggles of a Native Canadian Woman*, the fictionalized autobiographical account of a counter-culture protagonist's travels in BC, California, and Ontario. Like Pennier's work, Campbell's, Culleton's, and Maracle's writings reflect on the experience of being of mixed descent. However, unlike Pennier's, these three books largely focus on the gradual development of an activist consciousness in a pan-tribal urban environment. These works were part of the developing political movement among Aboriginal people in Canada during the 1960s and 1970s,[20] and most subsequent Aboriginal writing in Canada has followed in their footsteps, with Aboriginal writers being part of a youthful, supportive, artistic, and politicized community. The more elderly Hank Pennier was not part of such a community (in fact, he comments disparagingly on 'these dirty long haired hippies'! [23]).

But if Hank's work sits uncomfortably alongside Aboriginal activists' voices, it also fails to play the same chords as

West Coast Aboriginal autobiographies and life stories such as James Sewid's *Guests Never Leave Hungry*, and Charles Nowell's *Smoke from Their Fires*. Unlike the material selected in these two works, Hank's choice of subject matter was not directed by an anthropologist. Moreover, Hank's writing is more representative of the vast majority of Native people who were neither chiefs nor political activists. His political resistance, personal empowerment, and decision to write his story took place in a way very different from that chosen by these other Aboriginal writers. His autobiography, therefore, presents a perspective rarely seen in indigenous writing in this country. Just as Hank initially challenged Wyn Roberts's expectations, he continues to challenge us as readers.

Though *Chiefly Indian* was largely ignored by scholars (even David Brumble's comprehensive *Annotated Bibliography of American Indian and Eskimo Bibliographies*, which picked up several 'half-breed' biographies in more obscure places, missed this one), it did find an enthusiastic popular niche readership. Hank's descendants remember that distribution through the small independent Vancouver publisher was a problem (whereas Campbell's autobiography was published by McClelland and Stewart and Culleton's by Pemmican Press), and it seems that the volume circulated principally through an informal system of library-like personal loans. As a boy growing up in a small coastal forestry town in the 1970s, one of the authors of this introductory essay remembers his father enthusiastically lending his prized copy of *Chiefly Indian* to a succession of friends. Every few months the book was retrieved so it could be lent to another reader. In the end, that well-loved dog-eared copy found its way into the hands of the chief of the Sliammon First Nation.

Meanwhile, many expatriate West Coasters apparently received copies of *Chiefly Indian* as Christmas presents. We know this because not a few readers took Hank Pennier seriously when he ended his autobiography with the invitation 'P.S. Send me a letter sometime' (89). His son Henry Jr (known locally among the Stó:lō as 'Jumbo'), now an elder himself living in his mother's community on the Chehalis reserve, remembers how happy it made his father whenever a letter postmarked from Europe arrived telling Hank how much a reader had enjoyed his book. Such correspondence continued to trickle in well into the 1980s.

Hank was a widower and nearly eighty-seven when he passed away in 1991. Nineteen years had passed since the publication of *Chiefly Indian*, and the world was a vastly different place from what it had been in 1972, let alone 1904. The term 'half-breed' was no longer publicly acceptable and had been largely replaced in BC by 'non-status Indian.' The designation 'First Nation' and 'First Nations people' had yet to become widespread, but 'Aboriginal' was becoming common parlance, and challenging 'Native' as the identifier of choice among indigenous people. Hank was working on a second book when he died. Close relatives say it continued very much in the humorous tone and character of the first volume. It also reflected on the changes in Aboriginal politics and Native–newcomer relations over the intervening years, but specifics do not seem to be remembered. Unfortunately, the loose-leaf manuscript that Hank kept in a shoebox beside his bed was misplaced when Hank's possessions were distributed after his death, but his son Henry Jr continues to be hopeful that they were just tucked away by one of his nieces and will turn up someday. We share this hope.

In the fifteen years since Hank's death, his Stó:lō community created two of the largest and most comprehensive Aboriginal organizations in Canada: the Stó:lō Nation Society and the Stó:lō Tribal Council. Together, these closely aligned entities are involved in treaty negotiations with the Canadian and British Columbia governments, and in the interim have acquired jurisdiction to administer and deliver child and family services, employment training, education, and fisheries, among others to their nineteen member bands' citizens. The Halq'eméylem language – Wyn Roberts's initial interest – is today spoken fluently by only two female elders (Elizabeth Herrling and Matilda Gutierrez), but Hank, along with other Stó:lō elders, was instrumental in helping establish an orthography and word list that today serve as the heart of revival programs offered by Coqualeetza, the Stó:lō Nation Society, the Stó:lō Tribal Council, and several individual Stó:lō First Nations. Hank's nephew Clarence 'Kat' Pennier was elected in 2003 to the Stó:lō Nation's top political office – the Yewal Siya:m – with a four-year mandate to lead the Stó:lō people to restoring healthy communities and re-establishing a comprehensive system of self-governance. Kat acknowledges his uncle Hank as having been an important role model.

As these brief examples illustrate, Hank Pennier has left a proud and rich legacy, not only through this book, but through the family and friends he inspired. Hank refused to be held back by circumstances or how others saw him. 'Call me Hank,' he told his readers, asserting the right to define himself and to tell his own story, in his own way, on his own terms. Sitting by the window in his small house, he wrote his life story, and though it was an intensely individual story, it provides a profound set of insights into the lives of Aboriginal people. The final anecdote in his book is a joke about two indigenous men who become lost while hunting. They decide to do something about their situation 'white man style' and fire three shots into the air. Having done this several times to no avail, one tells his friend to fire again. 'I can't,' the other man replies. 'I haven't any more arrows left' (89). With this last story, Hank is not just leaving us with a laugh; he is also leaving us with a question. Will anyone hear him? He has decided to tell his stories 'white man style' – in English, in writing. But without the tools that many writers (especially non-Native writers) have – formal education, academic or literary role models, access to large publishers – could he make his story heard? Or would he, like the two lost men, be sending his message in vain? We hope that, in reissuing Hank's autobiography, we are helping others to hear his voice.

Keith Thor Carlson
Kristina Fagan

P.S. Although Hank is no longer with us, his son Jumbo wants readers to know that the family would still appreciate receiving a friendly letter from readers – or maybe an email.

Foreword to 1972 Edition

Early in 1969, after I had returned from a research trip to England, as a linguist I became interested in the possibility of doing work on the Salish Indian dialects in the Haney-Mission district of British Columbia's Fraser River valley, east of Vancouver.

The purpose was to try certain theories I had developed about Phonology,[1] a branch of my Linguistic discipline, against data from a language very different in its sounds, structures and grammar from anything I had studied previously. Dr. P.W. Davis, now of Rice University, Texas, was my colleague at the time, and he was working with an Indian, Richard Bailey, on the Haney Reservation.

I was an observer at several of the Bailey sessions and became fascinated by the old Indian stories of the legendary, god-like figures that he told. Then I began a search for my own informant but who would speak a form of Salish that would be different from Bailey's. It is called *Halkomelem*.[2]

Bailey and his wife took me to a small house on the Nicomen Trunk road, east of Mission, there to meet Henry Pennier who soon made it plain that his name was Hank. There was empathy from the beginning. We arranged that I would visit him for two hours each Sunday and, thanks to a grant from the President's Research fund at Simon Fraser University, the meetings progressed for more than a year, although not with the results I anticipated.

My purpose was to have Hank speak his language to me
either as simple words or as stories and I would record
them on a tape recorder. I would transcribe the notes later
using a phonetic script, since none of the Indian dialects in
this area seem to have a system of writing their own. As
explanation I told him simply I was after Indian stories and
as many Indian words as he could remember, for although
Hank is a half breed I had discovered he knew the language well indeed.

The following Sunday, I was disappointed to find he had
written me not an old Indian story but had prepared one of
his own out of his past (the great bear hunter, page 44) and
in English.

Again I explained my purpose and to my chagrin found I
was not going to get old Indian stories from Henry Pennier; that it would not be for me to unearth on the
Nicomen[3] another 'Raven' story. In any case I knew I could
learn a lot from him in terms of Indian vocabulary and I
suggested he think of words for animals, fishing, hunting,
etc., for the next Sunday. I added that if he had the time he
might think also of how his story in English might be translated.

For some strange reason I asked him also to write some
more stories that could be translated into *Halkomelem*. I
suppose this could well have been motivated by an unwill-
ingness to face defeat. If I could not discover old Indian
stories, maybe I could find new ones – a vanity I admit to.

There was a feast awaiting me on my next visit. He had
prepared not only a list of words and the story ready for
what I expected would be an oral presentation for recording, but he had also written both the story and the words in
a writing system that he had devised for *Halkomelem*. His system was a good one – not perfect phonetically, which is not
necessarily a criterion for appropriateness when it comes to
orthographies, but still fascinating and worthy of study.
Here is an example:

Tel le quah Ehew. Le gatat weet.
From a certain place North. There is a hunter.
Wholmough to ghla. t-whe cha kastatka cha se-la-lum.
Indian himself. Ninety and eight years.

Pennier's English version: There once was a Great Bear Hunter (an Indian aged about 98). He lived in the Northern parts (of British Columbia).

One point became clear: Hank Pennier was an intelligent man. He did not translate literally and he had a feeling for both Indian and English style. As well, it was apparent that he was comfortable with his spelling of Indian and he seemed to have an innate feeling for the use of roman letters for writing out his native tongue without letting their use for English, or French, influence him perversely.

In the next months things proceeded smoothly with Hank supplying me with lists of words and with working partly on my own analysis of the recordings and partly on working with him improving his orthography. His fluency in the latter was growing constantly and my own ability to use it was improving greatly to my satisfaction.

At the same time, the stories or vignettes came pouring out and I began to anticipate more the composition of the stories than I did to my accumulation of vocabulary and grammar. I found I was becoming more like Wilhelm Grimm than Jacob Grimm, the German philologists and grammarians who began as serious grammarians but ended with Wilhelm becoming more and more interested in collecting folk fairy tales than in their use for grammatical studies.

I began to love the subtle humour, the kind and optimistic nostalgia of the stories, their honesty and lack of pretension and a certain mystique in them that appealed to me – possibly because I am Welsh and like most Celts, find irresistible anything fey. In recounting some of the stories, many mentioned possible parallels with Will Rogers and

Harry Golden,[4] but as a comparative newcomer to North America those names meant little to me. I felt merely the appeal of the stories and that Hank Pennier was a man with a certain, special talent.

I determined the stories should be published somehow, somewhere. In contacting the *Vancouver Sun* with an idea they might be published weekly, I met Jack Richards. He turned down the idea but suggested that Herb McDonald, a publisher/author/photographer of West Vancouver might be interested. He was. I put the stories in his hand, he asked for more, travelled up the valley with me to meet Hank, made all the arrangements, assembled and smoothed lightly the stories into a chronological whole, and eventually brought a good idea, a Welshman's intuition and a half breed's talent to your hand now.

I hope this little book will be successful, not only commercially, but that it will bring some joy to those who read it. In my estimation the book reflects perfectly the spirit of the man and it would be redundant of me to try and encapsulate it into some nice academic sentence. In the long run, the book also says something about myself and the publisher but any way you look at it, this book *is* Henry Pennier.

E. Wyn Roberts Ph.D. (Cantab.)
Assistant Professor of Linguistics
Department of Modern Languages
Simon Fraser University
Vancouver, British Columbia
[1972]

Opposite: Map of Lower Fraser River place names mentioned by Hank

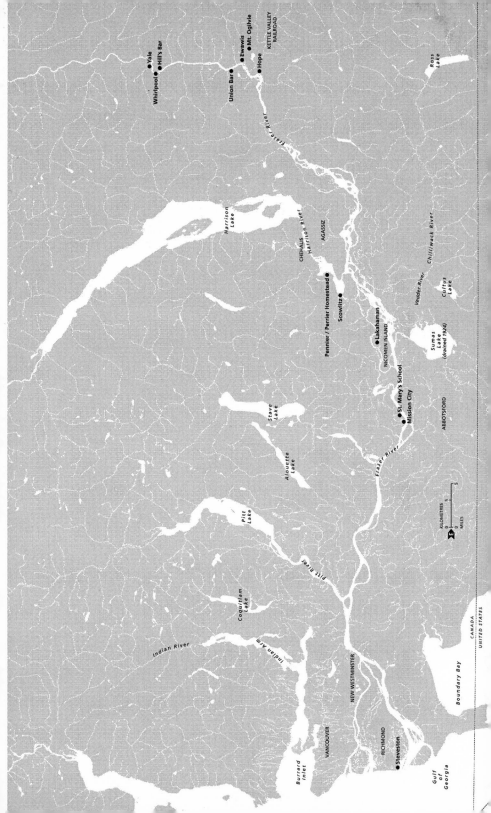

'CALL ME HANK'

Prologue to 1972 Edition

My name is Henry George Pennier and if you want to be a friend of mine please you will call me Hank.

I am what the white man calls a half breed. Even Indians call me half breed and why not since I have been one all my life from the time I was born in 1904 at a very early age.

I call me Pennee-err but my grandfather called himself Pennee-aye when he arrived in this here Fraser River Valley of British Columbia in the late 1870's, only it wasn't called British Columbia until later on.

I don't think I ever knew what my grandfather's first name was. All I can find out is that he was in some kind of good business in Quebec and he had a couple a partners there and once when he went back to French-Canada to check on them, one of them gave him lead poisoning in the back and killed him dead, leaving his Indian wife and my father George. Of course he wasn't my father then as he was a little boy.

As near as I can tell my father was her only child and he grew up on the family homestead on the Harrison River which is just a long eagle's glide from my place now.

Well, about 1890 my father George, he married a half breed by the name of Alice Davis. They had eight children and two died while they were babies. That left six of us to grow up and I was the youngest. Now I am the only one left.

I don't remember my father because he died the year I was born. I only remember my stepfather.

Then I got married in 1924 to Margaret Leon who is a Harrison River Indian[1] too except there is just a little Chinese in her somewhere back a piece. And we had Beatrice, Maisie, Henry, Perry and Irene but I can't remember in which order. Only Irene and Henry are living now and Renie has 11 children. And besides, from Maisie's daughter we have a grandchild.

And all of us are half breeds. Not white men and not Indian yet we look Indian and everybody but Indians takes us for Indian. It has been a complicated world and in some ways it still is I guess. And the damn government hasn't helped any.

I suppose you want to know about me.

Well, when I was a logger and working my ass off I was five foot eight and 147 pounds of muscle. Now I am five five and weigh about 200 pounds. And the reason is that a couple of bad logging accidents left me with two broken hips. Besides, I don't have a left knee cap anymore.

I shuffle around this little place of ours using a crutch on my right side and a cane on my left side but most of the time I just sit in this big chair by the window watching the ducks swoop in on the slough beside the house and I think and I keep remembering how it was.

I have had 13 years of it now and a man with nothing else to do can remember a hell of a lot in that time.

Then this guy McDonald showed up one day with a teacher friend of mine and he Irish talked me into putting it all down on paper. He sent me a bunch of foolscap pads and some pens and if what is printed here don't make much sense sometimes I guess it's because he couldn't make out my writing.

So like they say on TV – This Is Your Life Hank Pennier, and I hope you get the idea.

H.P.
Deroche, British Columbia

Part 1
I Remember My Kid Days

I was less than a year old when my dad had an accidental death while hunting in 1904. I had three brothers and two sisters and lucky the boys were the older ones so they helped out our mother quite a lot.

We lived in a wooden frame house, twenty-four by forty feet that was partitioned, and had an upstairs room. It was on a eight acre piece of a eighty-seven acre homestead adjoining the Chehalis Reservation on the Harrison River.[1]

There was an old wagon road down to the Chehalis settlement two miles to the south, then we took a canoe down the Harrison River. The Chehalis Indians were very kind and friendly neighbours to have.

When I was five we all went down the Fraser River a ways to Hatzic[2] to pick strawberries for a berry farmer and I can still remember the general store with all the candy that still stands there today.

I remember watching the old sidewheeler Beaver[3] blowing lots of black smoke and sparks come chugging up the river to the Hatzic Landing. Later on I learned she was the first steam boat on the whole Pacific coast. Then the bigger boys would get into their canoes and paddle out to meet her and get bounced around by the waves and swells the old Beaver made.

That was also the first time I saw a train. On clear nights sometimes back at the house you could hear her whistle a long ways off but this time at Hatzic was the first time I saw one close up. This young lad only a little older than me took me down to the Canadian Pacific tracks and he showed me how to lay down with my ear on the rail and pretty soon I could hear her coming. Then he took a quarter out of his pocket and put it on top of the rail. Boy was I scared when she went past. Then we climbed up the bank and picked up his quarter and she sure was squashed all out of shape. He gave it to me and I think it is still around some place.

From there next I knew, we were at the hop yards[4] at Agassiz, where Indians from all over the place gathered to pick the hops. In those days there was acres and acres of fine hop fields all over the valley for all the beer factories and they needed lots of labour at harvest time. Which was good for the Indians because they got a pretty good stake for their winter's food supply.

I suppose that's where my mother met this guy she married later. He was from a little settlement called Union Bar[5] on the Fraser River about three miles east or upriver from Hope in the canyon. He had a nice place and there was plenty of fruit trees but his house was smaller than our homestead one. He always planted a very nice garden.

You had to travel to Union Bar from Hope by canoe and that was tough because the current runs pretty good there and you had to paddle against it. In the freshet[6] season you had to pack the trail which was real snakey up on top of the canyon wall.

My stepfather took me to Hope sometimes and there was a Chinaman's store there and that was where I got to be so scared of those Chinese with their long pig tails. They would be smoking these long pipes when we would go into the store and they would reach out and feel my arms and cackle and say to my stepfather how much for the boy.

That was where I first saw my stepfather's dad. He was an old guy but he never had a whisker on his face. If a whisker popped out, out it came roots and all, with his little knife.

He was a nice old man and my brothers and sisters and I
saw quite a lot of him.

At night he used to tell us long stories of the past. Especially in the long winter evenings with us sitting around the
wood stove to stay warm we listened to him tell us about the
brave Indian warriors and spooky dead spirits and beautiful
Indian maidens and I guess that was when I started to be
proud I was a Indian or at least part of a one. If I was
smarter I would have listened a lot harder and learned a lot
more but of course I was still quite young.

The story I liked best was about the Yokoughltegh
Indians[7] from the west coast of Vancouver Island who were
known as the fiercest warriors on the whole coast of British
Columbia and farther south into what is now Washington
state.

They would work along the coast fighting and killing and
taking the odd slave such as a pretty young maiden or whoever they thought was fit and strong. Once in a while they
would venture up the Fraser River as far as Yale and on one
of those trips up that far they killed everyone except one
woman and her little son. Then they took off for the high
hills.

Where the massacre was was named Ewawis,[8] about two
miles east of Hope. Well, the mother, all alone, grew up the
boy to become an Indian doctor and you did not get these
spiritual powers without a lot of hard work. He became a
very powerful spiritual man.

That was just in time for the next bunch of war canoes all
loaded with warriors that came up the river. He was waiting
for them by the bank and as they passed he hypnotized
them with his great powers. Then he just waded out from
the bank to their canoes and while they all just sat there
hypnotized he clubbed each and every one of them to
death single handed.

How do we know this now? The Indians had a law of
their own and one was they would always leave two braves
alive. That's what the doctor did. He let two go and sent

them back home to tell their Chief what had happened. This is why most of the Indian stories of the past are true. There were always two survivors left to tell the story and pass it on. There was no telephone or newspapers or TV in those days.

The story we talked most about it seems now was about a certain whirl pool in the Fraser canyon part that only appeared during freshet and which even the stern wheelers[9] avoided. There was this brave who got sucked in, canoe and all, and his friends thought he was a goner for sure.

Then the next day or thereabouts the searchers heard hollering way way up on the mountain side and quite a ways down river from the whirl pool. Sure enough they spotted the brave way up on the sheer face of the rock in an opening of a cave. He couldn't have climbed up there it was so sheer. Not even a mountain goat could have got near the cave. It was a big job to rescue him by braiding up some long ropes and snaking them down from the top, but how he got up there after being sucked down into the whirl pool[10] is still a mystery to me.

It was scary stories like that I grew up on.

Boy do I ever remember my first trip to Hope. It happened on a very cold winter's day and the edges of the river were jammed with big hunks of ice with lots of pieces drifting by my stepfather's canoe.

Later on when I went to the Mission school[11] I learned about all the pioneer missionaries, most all Catholic, who travelled up and down the river in their canoes in such weather and even worse. We can class the Medical Doctor and the Missionary as two rugged individuals.

You take a Medical Doctor in those days. If someone was very sick and a brave came to tell him, whether there was a blizzard on or not he always made his call. He had to pack the trail or travel by canoe or ride his big horse. But they took all that in stride as part of their duty. Very kind and obliging doctors they were. Now I would have to be dying fast before I could get one to drive his big car a few miles from town out to my place here.

You take special days like Easter Sundays and Christmas and Holy Days, speaking of missionaries and travelling in bad weather and such. The Missionary would name a celebration meeting place, and such as the Port Douglas Indians[12] would travel by canoe all the way down the Harrison Lake which is forty-three miles long, to places such as Chehalis or Chilliwack or to the Indian Residential School at Mission City. Sometimes the weather would be so bad and the snow would be so deep and it would be so cold but if the missionaries could do it in the old days so could the Indians they said.

For the Indians on the coast from where Vancouver is now and farther up, their meeting place most always was Sechelt where there was a big wood church on the beach with a couple a high towers you could see from a long ways away. It only burned down a few years back.

That is where the big brass band competitions were. Did you know that in those days most all the bigger reserves had Indian brass bands? Oh yes. Much later on at the big yearly exhibition in Vancouver the Indian brass band competitions was something everyone looked forward to. Although none of them was educated too well, they sure could read their music notes, but I myself do not know one note from another. The missionaries sure must have had to get a lot of donation money to buy all those instruments for the young braves but I guess they thought it was a good way to do God's work.

Anyway to get back to my story of my kid days my brothers and sisters and myself were finally admitted into the Catholic Indian Residential School. As we were half breeds and we could not live on the reservation, we were supposed to be white and we came under the white man's status. But the priests were very kind and they made an exception in

our case. They went out of their way. It was the Oblate
School near Mission City and school was for eleven months
with August being the holiday time.

A little while after we went to stay there there was this
picnic on the grass out in front. I remember it was a nice
hot summer's day. As a rule the priest always sat at the head
of the table and being such a good boy I always got to sit
next to him. Everything was going along pretty smooth
until I passed him the salt. It wasn't in a salt shaker so I suppose he thought it was sugar, and he put a whole big tea-
spoon of it into his cup. I was watching him but since I
thought maybe he likes salt in his tea better than sugar I
didn't want to foul things up by saying anything so I kept
quiet.

He finally tested his tea and apparently it didn't taste
right so he put in more salt and stirred it and then took a
big drink. All at once his teeth started clattering and his
tongue stuck out at the same time. For a while I thought he
was going to swear at me but being a priest I suppose he
thought he had to control himself. But I didn't get to sit
beside him anymore.

Then a little later on I became a altar boy. I suppose you
want to hear some altar boy stories.

Every so often good old Archbishop Casey from Vancouver would make a trip up the valley to say mass at all the little mission churches. One time I was his altar boy at a
church on an island in the river near Agassiz. When it came
time for Holy Communion, as first altar boy I was ordinarily
the first to receive Communion. I genuflected and went to
the centre and held the napkin under my chin with both
hands, closed my eyes and stuck out my tongue and waited.
It seemed quite a while passed so I opened my eyes. When I
did there was Father Chirouse who was assisting, giving
Communion to the people at the railing behind me.
Apparently he forgot about me. I never did forgive Father
Chirouse for that.

You know about Ascension Day where there is the main

service at the big altar of the church. Then there are two or three temporary altars set up outside in different places and the whole congregation makes a procession behind the priest and altar boys going from altar to altar where there is a short service at each one. Well I was leading the procession and carrying high up so everyone could see it, the big, long iron crucifix. Then came this big Temptation. Since I was leading, all I had to do was make a little detour where I knew there was a long puddle about a foot deep and everybody would have had to follow. But I lost my nerve or maybe it was because I was able to resist Temptation. One thing I know is that when I got older I gave in more and more and I guess that's why I always seemed to have more fun than most. If the procession had followed me through it the people probably would have crucified me on my big iron cross. I was about the right size for it.

Another time when Temptation almost got me was when I was serving mass for a wedding. I had a big broken down man's ring in my pocket and the rhinestone had fallen out. There was nothing left but a big hole about a quarter inch in diameter. It came time for Father to bless the wedding band which was laying in the little silver platter I was holding. Then I thought of the one in my pocket. What a chance to make an even trade I thought. The old Devil must have been lurking around enticing me. I almost bust out laughing thinking about it. But I was able to resist Temptation again and every thing went like it was supposed to which should prove to you that I was a good Christian.

Then one time I was put in charge of about 10 boys around my age and we had a quota of seed potatoes to cut for the planting. Just before I was going to give the boys a few minutes rest I made up what looked like some thin wafers of potatoes with my knife that looked just like the Communion wafers that Father used during mass. Well I made the boys kneel down in front of me all in a line and as I was pretending to give the boys Communion I looked around and there was Father Rohr the Superior, standing there behind me. Boy o boy was I ever scared but I got by without being punished thanks to God.

Punishment was handed out by Father pretty severe in those days but some years later on I got a good lesson that words in a sarcastic tone sometimes worked even better. Another example I never forgot.

I guess I was about 17 and I was watching some bible slide pictures from a magic lantern that were being shown by a minister in a Hope church during his sermon. Things were going nicely except for this one guy and he was no kid either. He was a real show off acting smart. I think he was the town cop's brother and he sure thought he was top dog. A smarty alex type. Well the minister put up with him for quite some time and then the kid overplayed his hand. The minister instead of bawling him out, spoke to him very kindly. Would you close the door from the outside please, he said and that was all. Well I'll never forget the look on that punk's face when he left. I still think it was a worthy lesson.

I left the school at an early age and it wasn't my fault. This holiday time came when we had a month at home like I said before. I stayed with my eldest brother and I helped him cutting shingle bolts for a shingle mill all that time. You don't see much shingle bolts any more. First you cut down cedar trees about 15 inches in diameter maybe and then you would cut the log into five or six foot lengths. Then you would split that length two ways to make four quarter sections and these were called shingle bolts. The mill used the bolts from which to hand split the cedar shingles and then these were called shakes.

Anyways when my brother delivered the bolts to the mill he couldn't get our money right away for some reason. This went on for a long time. He was anxious to get the money because he wanted to get me some decent clothing to go back to school with. When I did get back to school finally I was over three weeks late and Father told me the school was all filled up. So I had to leave.

I was about 13 then, and after I got out things were never quite so nice again.

It was 1917 when I had to leave St. Mary's Mission City school and when I got off the train at Harrison Mills[13] where my oldest brother lived with his family because he was married by then, I found out he had joined the Army and had gone far away to England. So I didn't stay there very long. I moved up to the Chehalis area where my other brother lived and stayed with him for a few months before going down to Hope to go to the public school there.

It was the fall of the year up there. Boy, there were thousands of fishes of all kinds of different species all over the place in creeks and even in the sloughs. And there were lots and lots of trout. I spent a long time learning how to handle a canoe and it sure was awkward. I learned the hard way by falling overboard quite often. There were Indian boys three and four years younger than I was and they had no problems at all. But I never gave up and soon I could handle a canoe pretty good.

I took on any little job I could get like clearing or slashing brush, blasting and burning stumps. I started using stumping powder and blasting powder at this time and it was a good thing to my opinion because it gave me a sense of responsibility. It gave me more confidence in myself to take on bigger and better jobs more quickly.

On one of those jobs I learned another lesson. This farmer had several acres of turnips to be pulled and trimmed and there were four grown men besides myself. I was able to keep up with them row for row. We were told the pay was going to be 25 cents an hour. When we finished all the men got their right rate of pay. When my turn came the boss looks at me and he says half man, half price. So I got 12½ cents for all my work.

I was riding up and down some of the valley on the new railroad pretty good along about then which reminds me I almost forgot to tell you about how I watched it all along being built. The Canadian National Railway that is. It went along our side of the Fraser. Over on the other side was the Canadian Pacific Railway that was first to go down the canyon.

I guess it was about 1910 when I was six years old that the blasters and track layers first showed up in our district. I can remember and still hear the thump thump thump thump of the big steam pile driver echoing all down the canyon while it built the trestles and bridges. Then there were the little dump cars the men pushed along a thin steel track for dumping the rocks and fill. I remember watching the powder monkeys only I didn't find out for a long time what that meant, and didn't know I would be doing the same kind of work myself some day, as they loaded the dynamite charges under the rocks and stumps all along the right of way and done the blasting. I would hide behind a big rock and put my hands over my ears before the big explosions came.

And I remember all the men with packs on their backs. We were told they were hoboes only now I know they were just men looking for work. They would climb out from under the C.P.R. freight cars when the trains stopped at Haig Station directly across from Hope and there used to be a scowferry[14] that was rope-pulled across the river there. If a man wanted to cross over on the ferry to the C.N. side of the river so he could ask the boss about getting some work, he got charged two dollars. But if the hobo wanted to walk about two miles upriver on the C.P. tracks, to where the river is narrower, he could holler across and my stepfather would cross over in his canoe to fetch him for one dollar instead. Of course then he had to walk back again the two miles to where the work was going on, only this time he was on the right side of the river. But he saved a dollar and a dollar was a dollar.

There was a C.N. superintendent who hired this Indian woman to cross him over in her canoe and there was quite a freshet running. She had her little boy with her. The canoe swamped in a whirlpool and the woman got drowned but the super was able to save the boy and himself.

Then there was this high cable crossing maybe fifty feet above the river. A little cage hung from the cable and you got in and you pulled yourself across by a rope that was tied to both ends each side of the river. It even took pack horses across. Well it was Saturday night and some C.N. track layers wanted to go to Yale for some beer which was on the C.P. side. Coming back feeling pretty high, one of the guys fell out of the cage and dropped into the river which ran very swift there. There was nothing the rest could do but to forget him. They were in the bunk house still drinking when about four hours later the guy who fell out walked in. They all thought they were seeing a ghost, but he was real. I was telling this story to some guys a few years back and one of them, a Swede, says Hank, it's true, dammit, I was one of the crew in the cage.

At the beginning when they first showed up my sister and I were afraid of the hoboes and we used to watch them from behind a tree hoping they wouldn't see us and catch us. One day the two of us were catching fishes in a little creek beside the trail the hoboes took from being ferried across in our stepfather's canoe. We spotted one coming down the trail and we took off. My sister hid behind one tree and I hid behind another. To my luck there was a yellow jacket nest where I hid and I got stung and stung and stung all over. But I did not make a sound as I was more afraid of the hobo.

Then they built this big construction camp on the Union Bar reserve, could have been three hundred workers assembled there. I didn't know the different nationalities at the time but I understood there were Swedes and Italians mostly. I got in good with the camp cook and got quite a few cookies and such as time went by.

When they were building the camp they uncovered a lot of Indian burial ground or battle ground skulls and they were lying around all over the place. They were two different shapes. There was the round shaped skull of the Fraser River Indian and then there was the pointed skull of the West Coast Indian.[15] That was when I started to understand that Indians are not the same. My sister and I used to kick the skulls around like a football until our stepfather caught up with us. He gave us some punishment and then buried them in the Indian cemetery.

My stepfather and some of his friends made up a story about the hoboes and the Indians and the Canadian National Railway and how it got built across Canada ahead of schedule. I remember it very well. The hoboes did not like walking so the hoboes and the Indians had a peace pipe smoking pow wow and they joined forces on a plan to get the railroad built from coast to coast as soon as possible. At any time the work slowed down the Indians would make a warlike raid. But the Indians quite often over played their hand. Of course they couldn't help it because they had no special law to go by. But the hoboes were happy because the work was going according to the pow wow plan. So it wasn't long before the hoboes were riding the rods all across the country. You can give thanks to the Indians and the hoboes for the early completion of the railroad. I don't suppose the C.N.R. ever heard that story before.

Well now it is when I am 13 and 14 again and I had worked some after leaving the Mission school. Then I went to the public school at Hope and it was a two and a half mile walk along those self same C.N. tracks I had watched being layed that I made every day. It was a tough walk in the rain, there and back. And I had this one problem.

There was a Indian cemetery right beside the tracks. There was this rocky bluff about twenty feet high above the tracks and the cemetery was right there on top, out of my sight. This scared me all the more because I never did trust anybody dead or alive, specially dead. And every little while the rails would make clicking sounds which now I know was expansion and contraction, but it didn't matter any then. I grew older every day from fear and today, almost sixty years later, I still shudder about it. I survived thanks to God for giving me strength at the time.

Speaking of dead people reminds me of a wake I was taken to about this time. There was this lady who was in charge of looking after things and giving people sandwiches and things who came. But a cousin of the deceased came by C.P.R. train from Vancouver quite late that night and he wanted to have one last look at his dead cousin. So the lady lifted the cover off the coffin and boy oh boy, but the dead man's nose was flattened sideways. All the friends were crying and carrying on but the lady couldn't stop herself from laughing. She covered her face with her apron and the other people thought she was crying also. The dead man's nose flattened out looked so funny. Apparently whoever made the coffin made it too shallow.

Walking up and back the C.N. tracks like I did to school I got to know quite a number of old timers. There was Old Lame Jack who was a bachelor in his late 80's and was quite strong. There was a church along the way and a playing field next to it and the Indians' houses were around it so as to be near to the church. I guess it was sort of a missionary rule. Old Jack would go and sit in the middle of this field almost daily, an hour or so before supper time and he would watch for the first smoke coming out of any house chimney. That is where Jack would visit because he knew that supper would be ready there first and that is how he got most of his suppers. Remember the lesson. Always watch for the first smoke.

Then there was this Mr. Webster who decided to make apple cider but didn't have a clue. He had a good orchard and he picked the apples very carefully and filled his hogshead barrels with them thinking the apples would form into cider by themselves. He covered the hogsheads and stored them away for a few months. At Christmas time when he had a visitor he went to tap the barrels and he got a pitcher and a couple a cups ready to drink the cider.

When he took the cover off to his astonishment the apples were still whole and firm, no cider. Well, he said to his friend, there won't be any headaches tomorrow. That was another good lesson. Don't count on anything or anybody and you won't be disappointed.

By now there was conscription for services in the war and a couple a guys cornered my brother in downtown Vancouver somewhere along Hastings street, my second brother that is. He said he couldn't join up and they said why. You guys watch me walk he said. And he chose the shortest distance to the corner and when he got there he started to run and they never saw him again. They must have been quite lax in their laws in those days. I remember another guy who was double jointed. All he had to do was put his thumbs out of shape. He also got by with that. The lesson I got out of that story was to be always cleverer than the next guy.

Running reminds me of the annual July 1 sports day on the Chilliwack reserve. It was called Dominion Day in those days and I always liked the sound of Dominion of Canada. Now they have changed it. Why don't the damn government never leave well enough alone? Anyways besides the running races of course there was the canoe racing and lacrosse and soccer and chasing the greasy pig and what have you. There was also the mosquitoes too. Boy do I remember those on Dominion Day sports days.

So they were having the foot races and the crowd wouldn't stay back off the course. My brother was on the racing committee and he went down by the slough and got himself a two foot snake which he put in his pocket. Then when the crowd still would not back up he yarded poor old Mr. Snake out and started swinging it around and the crowd sure did back up and get off the course then. I always liked snakes a little better after that.

That was the same day I got up enough nerve to fight this big bully who was always picking on me. I told him straight you better be careful because I'm so clumsy if I start swinging my arms about I might hit you in the face. So he charged me and I swung and I just happened to connect. Boy was I surprised. There was only two hits, once when I hit him and once when he hit the dirt. I think that was the first time I learned to really stand up for myself.

Well, in the summer of 1918 in Hope I picked up any odd little chore I could get ahold of and things were going along pretty nicely until the Asian Flu Epidemic[16] hit the valley and people started dying all over the place. Whether you were white or Indian or old or young or rich or poor didn't seem to make any difference. When your turn came you had to go. You couldn't buy your way out.

There was liquor prohibition[17] in British Columbia then and you had to get your booze by prescription from the drugstore as it was supposed to be used like medicine only. My brother-in-law had a prescription for a small bottle of whiskey but I don't suppose it mattered much. Whiskey helped some and didn't help others. There were all sorts of rumours and no one really knew what was going on.

My mother was acting as a nurse going from door to door wherever she was needed most. She even was a midwife once. The lady was down with the flu but my mother was able to get both she and her child to survive but the husband he died.

Finally my two sisters and I we all got it and then she had to look after us. One of my boy friends got it and just before he died he had a long bad nose bleed. Well when my nose started to bleed and kept on for a half an hour I thought I was a goner for sure.

And in all those weeks she was mingling with these sick people the old flu bug never did get to my mother. It was finally decided that her smoking a pipe protected her.

After that in Hope things got pretty slow. Of course being a half breed I couldn't go onto a reservation and be looked after a little bit. I was fifteen years old and there was only one thing to do, keep moving and find some work.

So I moved back up to the Harrison area again and

started slashing and clearing some land for this big rancher. There wasn't much money in it but it was something to do. Then in August there was four weeks of hop picking at Agassiz. I had a partner but despite our working hard the both of us we couldn't save any money. Trouble was we got our pay daily by means of a ticket which could only be cashed in at the hop yard store so that place got all our money back, but since there was so many different people from all over the valley we had lots of fun anyway.

And that is about the end of my growing up kid days because the next year in 1920 I started to work in real earnest.

Now I am sitting here in my chair with this paper and pen on the table and I am looking across the field to a mountain up against the valley which is the same place I grew up in. And I wonder I say to myself which time was best when I was a boy. And you know I think it was when I was 12 when I went with two hunters up old Ogilvie Mountain right to the top and for the first time I saw what was on the other side.

Ogilvie Mountain is about the highest peak you can see around Hope, directly back of Kawkaw Lake. It took us a whole day to get to the base and it was pretty rugged going. The next morning early we started up the mountain and a little way up they told me to wait in a little bald place while they took off in different directions to find game. Sure enough they jumped old Mr. Mountain Goat and he came running down the ravine about fifteen feet from me but I couldn't do anything since I didn't have a gun.

Then after a while we got way up to the top and looked over on the other side. Boy it was pretty. There was a vast meadow of the mountain blueberry, a very sweet kind that wasn't at all like the blue huckleberry I had been used to. There must have been hundreds and hundreds of acres up there. Nothing but blueberries. Then I found two kinds of wild raspberries, the red and the yellowish kinds.

And whistlers. Boy there were hundreds. They are a sort

of rock rabbit and they came out of the rocks and whistled at us and then ducked back in. Then we spotted this mother bear and her two cubs down the slope dining on the blueberries and Frisco snuck down to make the kill. His first shot wounded Mrs. Bear and did she ever become violent, but he downed her with his second shot. While we were skinning her Frisco looked around and there were the two cubs sitting watching. Frisco said they were big enough to make out for themselves so we didn't bother them. When we cut into a hind quarter there were white worms right in the flesh and I promised myself then and there no bear meat for me. No sir.

I sure felt all Indian that day though.

Part 2
I Remember My 1920s Days

I was 16 in 1920 when I got my first job in the bush. It was with a little camp at Othello[1] about five miles east of Hope on the C.P.R.'s old Kettle Valley branch line. It crossed the Fraser at Hope and then ran up beside the Coquahalla River into the mountains heading for the Merritt district. That old line is long gone now but she sure was one fine piece of railroading in her day and I sure didn't like the C.P.R. much for abandoning her. But I suppose business is business.

My job was wheeling sawdust. It was a rail tie and rough lumber mill and it cut maybe 12,000 feet a day. There were about 30 men and there wasn't any commissary store.[2]

What made things just right for me was there was this train going into Hope every night just after supper time and another that left Hope at 11 p.m. headed out past the camp. The fare was 20 cents each way. So I used to go to Hope almost every night to get snuff and tobacco and other kinds of supplies for the loggers. Most all would give me the train fare with their orders so I always ended up with lots of extra 20 centses. In fact I made a pretty good profit.

I worked in that camp for a whole year and I had my own wooden bunk in the bunk house and my own wash basin and blankets and tick which was what we called a straw filled mattress.

Once the boss gave me a long envelope with papers to get signed at the Hope station. It was a bill of lading for a carload of lumber. On my way back to camp that night I had my pockets so stuffed with tobacco and such for the men I lost the envelope. When I told the boss about it boy was he ever furious and he made me walk the tracks all the way back to Hope next morning to get a copy of the damn letter. Five miles there and five miles back.

You know now when I think about it all and the way I worked to get ahead and get a little money and maybe just survive in those kid years and then I read about these dirty long haired hippies today wandering around and taking government welfare money with all the jobs there is to do still, I wonder what's happened to the world. Being a half breed I had to fend for myself but now I don't think I would have taken dole money if I had been offered it.

Anyways Saturday nights were the best nights for me. Hope had two saloons and those Swede loggers and fallers would wander around between them for their booze. Every time I would meet one he would give me some small change as I was their sort of mascot, and I'd have quite a nice stake before the night was over specially on pay days. After they had got pretty likkered up they always were more kind-hearted and free.

Hope was a thriving little town then with four sawmills around it, lots of prospectors and lots of train men. On Sundays there would be baseball games and all sorts of activities. And quite often on Sundays I used to visit a friend about my age and his stepfather would send us down to the hotel with a gallon bucket to get draft beer for him. He had a standing order so we had no trouble getting it. Of course on the way back we would sample it now and then. Who wouldn't. It was only two per cent stuff.

There was lots of deer and blue grouse and good fishing where the mill was at Othello that was in this valley that was the shortest route from Hope to Princeton. And that was the route the horse dealers always took driving the horses from the Interior down to the Fraser Valley and on to Vancouver.

I remember one horse trader called Normie. There was some cabins along the trail for night time stopovers and the guy a few miles ahead of Normie stopped at one and then went sound asleep on the earth floor. It was dark as the ace of spades when Normie herded his horses up to the same cabin on his hands and knees. He lay down straddling this guy cross ways. The guy woke up and he thought it was a bear and the fight was on, fighting for their dear lives in the darkness. Finally one of them coughed and they were so busy defending themselves neither guy got hurt. When Normie told me about it he said he had never been so scared before.

Speaking of horse dealers reminds me about the big wheel type I saw in Hope in a saloon and he was chewing snuff. Spitting was quite an art in those days and some could make the old brass spittoon ring at six or seven paces without missing once. But this big wheel didn't know about spittoons I guess so he spit on the floor. The barkeep would move the spittoon in that direction but then the guy would spit some wheres else. So then the spittoon would get moved to that place. This went on a long time and finally the big wheel got mad. He said dammit, if you don't take that darn thing away from me I'll spit in it. Spitting is sure a forgotten art.

And I mustn't forget to tell you about an old Frenchman friend of mine at Harrison Mills who sold a horse that was blind in one eye. When he was making the sale he told the guy this is a damn good horse but it don't look good. So the guy bought the horse and as he was leading it into his stable the horse bumped the door. That was when he found out the horse was blind in one eye and he made the Frenchman go to court. When the judge heard the evidence that the Frenchman had told this guy that the horse didn't look good, he said the Frenchman had told the truth and so the Frenchman won the case.

Next year when I was 17 I drifted back to Chehalis because there was a good prospect at a logging camp. In the meantime while waiting I went back to my old standby clearing land and stumping.[3] By this time I had three other lads working for me and we had more fun than money. Besides which I didn't have to work so hard.

The following year was 1922 and the job I got in the logging camp I was after was the start of my career as a logger. It was really my third year in the woods and the job was as a hook tender which was one of the better type jobs. I even done a bit of high rigging.

One day I remember standing in the line at the time keepers office who also looked after all the minor replacements such as files, axes, ax handles and such. This big faller in front of me says to the time keeper I want a methodist ax. The time keeper says a methodist ax? What kind a axe is that? The faller says one of those two faced ones. Of course what he meant was a double bitted axe. I guess if you are a methodist you won't like that story. I am sorry because I have never said anything about somebody else's religion. I guess methodists are pretty good too.

Then there was this steam donkey engine which we called a steam pot that a crew was using to load a car with logs out of the lake. It was an old pot and while they were working the boiler part blew up. The two loaders took off. One ran along the shore with his peevee hook in his hand. He stopped and looked back and he saw the steam still spouting and he just kept on running. The other loader took off for the tall timbers and nobody saw him again for four days. As for the poor loading engineer who was standing next to the steam pot when she blew up I never did hear what happened to him. He maybe still flying around in Heaven for all I know. Anyway he didn't have to work no more.

So now I want to tell you about my lacrosse days as I sure loved that fast game. A lot of us young fellows formed a

club and some had played the game before. There were a
lot of teams around the valley by then, a lot of them were
Indian. Chilliwack Landing and Chilliwack Township and
the Sardis Indians[4] all had real good clubs.

What they play now is box lacrosse and that is a lot different from field lacrosse in the old days. We didn't have any
pads and helmets and protection like that, not even gloves.
The field was the same size as a football field not the little
dinky thing they use now, and there were no boards to play
a rebound off of. There were twelve men to a side and no
extras or substitutes, and what you did you just got out
there in the open sun and you ran and ran and ran all the
time and if a man got hurt bad that was it. Then one team
played a man short. If the two men got hurt then the team
played two men short. I have known some games when
there were only half a dozen men left on the field. I also
remember one time when a man played all the second half
with two broken ribs because he didn't want to let down his
side. You had to be good and wiry and fast and tough specially tough when those sticks started whacking into your
ribs and legs. You see the way these boxla guys are padded
up now and they get into a fight? Hell with protection like
that where is the fun? It isn't the same game anymore.

It was the free for alls the spectators enjoyed and a lot a
times they were in there fighting as well. I remember once
a crippled white guy was right in there with his crutches
slashing at anyone in range and when the smoke cleared
his crutches were all broken up. The Sardis and the Township teams were real rivals and when a couple a their players got into a fight we managed to get them stopped and to
postpone the fight until after the game. So the game continued with everybody tensed up and ready to fight at the
drop of a hat. I remember the ref sure had his hands full
that day. Somebody got a pair of boxing gloves and after
the last quarter we all formed a ring right there in the middle of the field. It was a very good fight and they settled

their argument fair and square and then were all ready for the next game.

We were in a game at the Fair Grounds with the Chilliwack Landing team and a fight started and the spectators joined in. I never did like to fight because they say it is hard on the eyes. So I went to the side line and a really big guy from the other side must have snuck around behind me and was going to let me have it when someone hollered. I looked back and ducked at the same time and he missed me. Right there and then this big spectator grabbed him and held him and at the same time someone else grabbed me from behind and locked my arms. In my heart I was glad but I knew I had to make a showing and I was sort of jerking myself away from this guy. Let me at him let me at him I kept shouting, but I wasn't pulling myself hard enough to get away. All the other fights stopped to watch what they hoped maybe would be the main event but it didn't materialize and the game went on.

Once when we were playing Sardis there was a guy named Sam. He thought he was going to get some property from his mother and he made a bet with her, $500 against this property. Sam had two brothers playing for the Sardis team. Sam's mother told me about the bet so I told her she didn't have to cross her fingers and that I usually had an extra card up my sleeve. I had to keep both eyes open that game because it was a rough one and very fast. It was sort of a see saw affair until the last quarter and near the end I got this card out of my sleeve and went to work. My plan was to make the winning goal and I did. As soon as I scored I send a smoke signal to my defence guys to guard our goal with their lives and they did. So it was a hard game but I made it easy and the old lady was $500 richer. I was all battered up but it was well worth it.

I used to do a lot of grandstanding just in order to annoy the opposing teams' morale. It was so simple and it always worked. They would get angry and then I'd go to work. Once during another Sardis game they had a guy from our district playing defence and he shot the ball into his own goal. They gave him heck but it didn't matter very much because the score was 9 to 2 in our favour.

That was the same game I had two right-footed running shoes on. Boy I couldn't run a straight line that game as both shoes were pointing the same way and that also worked in my favour as the defence men thought I was going to pass them on their left side all the time. When I had left the camp to play I grabbed two right shoes. Simple reason but it sure worked out funny.

Worst game ever I was in was against the North Vancouver Indian club and we played at Brockton Point in Stanley Park, Vancouver. They were all older and more experienced and they sure showed us up. Their strategy was to sluff around until we followed suit and then all at once to break out of it and score. We got murdered. It was a bad day and after all these years I still shudder when I think of it.

When our team broke up because we got short of players I joined the Chilliwack City team and we done very well but did I ever get it being an Indian, or at least looking like one, playing with a white man's team again two different Indian clubs. They treated me very rough but I enjoyed it the more they hit with that old hickory stick because I then scored more goals. The Indian spectators sure gave me the works and they called me all sorts of names like white man born in a smoke house and lots more that you wouldn't print. But I got a kick out of it as long as we were winning games.

Well now I watch a soccer game sometimes but when they get slow I have to think of something to make it worth while. So here's the answer I found and maybe it will work for you. Every time I go I take some whiskey with me and when the game gets slow I take a good slug and things start to speed up pretty good. Another slug and then the game gets faster. Because as far as I'm concerned it doesn't matter who wins as long as it's good and fast since I always do enjoy a good fast game.

I played a little baseball too but not much. I was watching this game between two good clubs and one was short handed so I was asked if I would fill in. They had me play second base. It wasn't a world series but it was a very good game. Luckily the ball hardly came my way so I got by pretty good. Then at the beginning of the 9th the score was all tied, the opposition was at bat and there were two out when the batter hit one right at me. I must have held my hand too rigid and I got him out but my left hand was almost too sore to work for two weeks. We managed to get another run so we won the game. They wanted to sign me up as a regular but I said I was too busy logging and the best part was nobody knew I had a sore hand.

And I was a pretty good swimmer too. One Sunday afternoon I went down to a little beach on the Harrison River to swim and there were two young lads swimming. I sure did love candy and I had a pound bag of chocolates with me from the camp's commissary store. I gave the boys a couple chocolates each and said there should be a diving contest and the rest of the chocolates would be the prize for the one who could stay down the longest. They both dived down together. It wasn't very long before one of them popped his head out and I motioned him down. Pretty soon the second one he pops up and I motion him down also. And this went on for quite a few minutes. When the boys caught on I divided the chocolates between them, they called it a draw and everybody was happy. I guess that just goes to prove there is a little crook in everyone, even an Indian.

Something else I did that year while I was at that camp was at night to fish for salmon on the Harrison by torch light. On this night I was paddling up stream ready to go into the mouth of Chehalis Creek and I noticed a little fire smouldering at the edge of the creek. As I got closer all at once the camp firelight flared up and then there were others appeared. About a dozen of these flames or lights travelled up the edge of the river moving fast, blinking on and off. They went upriver about 100 yards and then moved back to where they started from and then they disappeared. I bet all the hair on my head were standing straight out. And there were the firework-like flames that have been seen more than once coming out of the Indian cemetery on the bank of the Harrison. I sure would like someone to explain it all, but the Indian explanation is quite simple. Ghosts!

In 1923, still working at the camp and doing so good I was able to buy me a little inboard motor boat and I guess that was my downfall, because the boat was the reason I met Margaret my wife. It was just like today when a guy gets a car so he can meet up with some dame. It seems to always work.

In 1924 there was a long winter shut down at the camp and nothing more could be done there until the old river rose in the late spring so we could get the logs in the river. So I went back to the old reliable, the stump ranch.

And on December 9, 1924, when I was 20, I signed the life long contract for better or for worse. Which meant I really had to work for the rest of my life. Funny part of it all is we were born on the same month, same year, baptized on the same day, got married the same day and we got our first child the same day. And soon. And we didn't go on any honeymoon either.

The next year I started up at the camp again at spring run off time and in August me and the wife moved to the hop yard camp at Agassiz so she could pick hops to earn extra money while I kept on working at the camp.

I forgot to tell there was one August when I got a job at the Sumas yard and there was about 700 pickers, Indians from all over the country. Some of the elderly ones would start picking at day break and so as to be fair to everybody as there was so many pickers my job was patrolling the fields, keeping the pickers off until seven in the morning. Boy that was the worst job I ever had because it was next to impossible to keep them away from the vines. They'd bawl me out in their own languages and I'll bet my last bale of hay there was seven or eight different Indian languages there. The job was getting me down since with my regular day's work, I was because of the patrolling working 13 hours a day at least. So I bought a bottle of 40% Jamaica rum because that was about the only good thing about being a half breed, I could buy liquor. Not all the time. Just sometimes. I thought it would help the cause along. This one morning long before day break I had a couple a hot rums and then a couple more for good luck and when I got out to the field I lay down on a pile of hop sacks to wait for morning and I must have fell asleep. And when I woke up about 5:30 there must have been a hundred or more out there all around me picking away like mad. Anyway I got away with it. Nothing was said.

There was a good sized hall and there was a couple a dances a week and we danced the charleston and the chicken scratch. Lots of fun. Well, I was out there dancing quite a lot and put on a sweat so I reached in my pocket for my handkerchief to wipe my face and instead I pulled out one of my wife's stockings. The darn thing was hanging down full length when I got to raise it up. There must a been a hundred and fifty eyes there looking at me and I sure was embarassed. I told my wife later she was never to put her stockings in my pocket again and she didn't. Now when I think of it she has been a damn good wife.

Quite a lot of the guys got broke through gambling and there was one clever guy I knew who needed money bad. He spotted two young boys about nine and he said to the first kid, you see that kid over there, he says you're a coward and afraid to fight. So working fast, he goes to the second kid and says, that kid over there says you're a momma's boy and won't fight and that was all it took. The people gathered around and the fight was on and George which was what his name was, called for the people to donate money to those kids that were putting on such a good show. They started tossing dimes, quarters, nickels into the circle and when there was quite a lot of change on the ground, George he gathered up all the money, stopped the fight and gave each kid a quarter. Everybody was happy. Specially George.

There was a R.C.M.P. officer stationed at the camp and he had his hands full with all the bootlegging that went on. And this young half breed turned stool pidgeon and ratted on one of the bootleggers. Well he sure got the old western treatment you can bet. The camp watch man and a few of the boys from Lillooet arranged a fake hanging as it was getting dark one night. They went down the road to a big pear tree and waited with their ropes and when the watch man told the stoolie to get out of camp fast and never come back and he was running down the road the cowboys lassooed him. They roughed him up considerable all done silently. They put the noose on his neck and then waited awhile. Finally one of them says lets give the buggar another chance if he promises never to stool again. Which he did. So they turned him loose and went chasing him down the road. I'll bet he's still running.

Speaking of booze reminds me to tell you about these two fallers that shipped out of Black's Loggers Agency in Vancouver, and they pooled what little money they had and bought half a gallon of rye. They were going to double their money when they got to camp by bootlegging the stuff. They shook hands and promised each other there will be no drinks served unless the drink was paid for by cash. At that time the loggers used to travel up and down the British Columbia coast by the Union Steam Ships, a slow means of transportation. So one of them got dry and wanted to have a drink and he took out a quarter and paid his partner for a slug. Pretty soon the other guy got dry and he bought a drink from the first guy with the same quarter. So it went until the jug was empty. No profit.

Then I remember George King, a hook tender, only we called him B.S. King. He buys two gallons of rum and ships out of Vancouver on his way to a camp up the coast. In those days some of the outfits paid cash instead of by check so some of the boys were quite stakey. When B.S. got to the camp he opened a gallon and treated the boys free. They all got feeling high so B.S. started selling the second gallon and he cleared 450 dollars. They would give him a ten or a twenty for a drink and he would keep the change. I don't think I would have the nerve to try that one.

By this time back at the camp, I was a choker man for a while and I gotta tell you about my friend Bones. Bones the Snoose Eating Logger.

He was a great big mongrel dog and he was so thin he was called Bones. He followed me to work one day and at lunch time around the steam pot where there were maybe a dozen of us he gobbled up the crusts we threw away from our sandwiches. He never missed a working day after that rain or shine. As the whistle would blow and we would get back to work Bones he would come too. And like I said I was a choker man then so I suppose you want to know what that is.

Well a choker man has a tough job for one thing. After a tree is cut down and is just lying there it was his job to poke a hole under the tree so that a big steel cable can be pushed through and then made into a sling. Then the sling is hooked to another big cable attached to the winch that runs off the old steam pot. Then the log is dragged back through the slash to gradually build up a big storage pile at a centre location. The pole that stood up in the middle of this pile that held the sheaves for the pulling cable was called a spar tree.

So now wherever there was supposed to be a choker hole dug I would poke a hole with a big stick and then Bones would take over and dig out the rest of the way for my cable. Then I would give Bones a chew of snuff only we called it snoose. Choker set, everybody in the clear, I'd hit Bones a little on the back and he'd yelp loud and the whistle punk would hear it, which was the guy operating the donkey engine, and he would start her up and pretty soon there was another turn of logs gone in. Between Bones and I we chewed up a can and a half of snoose a day.

Then the camp shut down for a month and when I came back Bones ignored me. He would not even look at me and I suppose he thought I had fired him. I would not have fired him for anything in the world. He was a damn good logger.

Another dog I remember belonged to Charlie the trapper and he came from northern British Columbia. Charlie made a very good catch this one winter and he makes over three thousand dollars when he sold all his pelts. He hadn't had a drink in a long long time so he decided to visit some beer parlours in Vancouver and have a few. He turned his whole dog team loose except his one favourite before he come to the city. I forget what he called that dog. So he brings the dog to the city with him and he ties it outside the beer parlour when he goes inside. It wasn't very long before all the dogs from the neighbourhood were all around the place causing quite a racket. Someone phoned the police and when the policeman got there of course Charlie had a few under his belt and nothing mattered much.

When the cop walked into the beer parlour he says whose dog's tied outside? Charlie says my dog. The cop says your dog's in heat. No Charlie says my dog eat already, I fed him dry fish this morning. You don't understand says the cop. Your dog wants ... and he makes some motions with his hands trying to make the Indian understand what he was trying to tell him. Oh sure, says Charlie, go ahead, long time I want police dog.

Then there was this friendly collie dog that belonged to a friend of mine at Hatzic and while he was talking to a visitor this fine summer day the collie started wagging its tail and dammit all at once his tail fell off. They were both quite shocked. They investigated and found out that some child had put a big elastic band to the base of the poor dog's tail and it looked like it had been on so long the tail just rotted away. Of course the dog was only a country dog and did not care about his looks probably. Anyway it didn't bother to grow another tail.

So the next year, 1925, I learned to play the fiddle for square dances and such and I even called for the square dances occasionally. This wasn't anything special because most of us guys could play the fiddle and guitar by ear that is. We had some wonderful times and in most cases we would dance until daylight.

Things seemed so different in those days. The air was fresher. There was none of this air pollution. The bird song seemed chirpier and happier and their music was all around. Of course there was this bit of rain, and sometimes there was snow mixed with it and then when it snowed real good and hard we did exactly as they do in Switzerland. We just let it snow.

Back at the hop yards again that summer was where our first child was born. So I celebrated and I bought a bottle of rum. Forty proof Jamaica. On account of so many Indians at the hop yards the place was temporarily named a reservation and so liquor was restricted. Being a half breed of course I could drink but not on the reservation. So the R.C.M.P. constable found us drinking and I wasn't quite sober so I got pinched. But both the Judge and the cop were very nice. When I told the Judge my story he thought it was a pretty good excuse so I got off.

In 1926 I was still a choker man and I bought me a Tin Lizzie, a 1923 Model T Ford. We worked six days a week and most all the roads were dirt. On Sundays I'd put on my Sunday best a blue suit and we would go for a drive. By the time we got home I would have a grey suit instead of a blue one on account of all the dust. But at least I had a car. It wasn't everybody that had a car in those days I can tell you.

Boy do I remember the first time I drove it and I hit a cow that was crossing the road. I couldn't seem to get the old Ford stopped and I was just barely moving when I hit her, sort of shoved her sideways a bit. The worst I could have done was to curdle her milk a little. Anyway she walked away with a smile on her face so I knew everything was in order. I didn't know whether she was making fun of me or being happy for herself.

'27 and '28 were very good years in the woods as far as earning money was concerned. But boy oh boy logging was a tough and rough game. You had to work or else. If you were a little slow getting to those chokers the hooker would holler at you, don't run, fly. And if you didn't down the road you'd go for your time card. Many's the guy who was packed out of the woods and I helped the odd one pack out too.

There was one new choker man in particular, he started work in the morning. Before noon on that day there were two of the boys injured. If this is logging he says, to hell with it, I'm quitting. And he did. If you worked overtime all you got was straight time. No time and a half about it.

We had a big 12 x 14 steam unit by this time, for yarding the logs in with and I remember this high ball wood's foreman standing behind the yarder engineer who was running her at three-quarter throttle. The Bull of the Woods finally got so he couldn't stand it any longer and he shouts to the engineer this thing's got only two speeds, wide open or shut. So the engineer sure punished that old yarder after that.

Nothing mattered just so long as they got the logs out. They were all log hungry. Specially after a few beers those high ballers would start those big logs flying around and you sure had to watch yourself and stay in the clear or you would get hit good, injured or maybe killed.

In the spring of '29 we got a new woods foreman who was a nice sort of guy very well liked by the men. One thing which interested me the most about him when the guys who would quit for a week or 10 days and then come back trying to get back on, he would give them their job back. He enjoyed helping fellas I think but of course you had to be a good worker in order to get away with this. Well one day I asked him about this method and his answer was quite simple. They have to work some place he says.

If you spoke to any foreman or any of the top brass too often instead of the rest of the crew calling you a teacher's pet or something to that effect, you were called a meat hound and a lot of other phrases I would not like to see in print because the loggers' language was pretty rough. Yes I guess meat hound is about the only one I can use here just now.

Well we logged most of the season. Same old routine. Men coming and going. The boys moved quite a lot, from camp to camp, and we called them the camp inspectors. There was Eight-Day Wilson and eight days was his limit in any one camp up and down the coast.

Well in the fall part of '29, one day we all went to work as usual in the morning, all of a hundred men or so. We did the usual good day's tough work and about an hour before quitting time there came around this guy to tell us the camp was shutting down that day right there and then.

The Bull of the Woods told me to watch over the loading of the 9 x 10 steam pot which I had been using for log loading. The train crew shunted me up the Bull car and I had it loaded in pretty good time. We threw our beaten up old gloves away and that was it. Everything else was left out there in the woods. Three steam cold deckers. The big 12x14 steam unit. And the big 7 drum skidder all in their settings, lines strung out and everything. Just left it there to rust. Just left it all there. The company had gone broke and there were no explanations.

It was all pretty damn sad and now when I think of it it still makes me sad so to cheer me up instead I will now tell you about Ollie the Swede who was one of the best and most noted high ball loggers in British Columbia in the late '20's. I never knew him but I sure heard enough about him. Anyways Ollie would just get down to Vancouver from some place in the bush and right away some boss logger would phone him to go back to work some place else. Ollie had no time for himself at all. Finally he smartened up and whenever he registered in a big Vancouver hotel he would sign himself as Dr. Ollie.

Well one night this woman got caught unexpectedly and had to berth a child right in her hotel room. The manager got a doctor for her but this doctor had difficulty so he figured surely there must be a doctor in a big hotel like this one. The manager went through the register and sure enough there was Dr. Ollie. So they got Dr. Ollie out of bed and up to this lady's room and the snoose eating logger sized up the situation. No problem at all he said. Dr. Ollie just sprinkled a little Copenhagen snuff into her nose and she sneezed and that was it. I guess whoever it is which makes that Copenhagen snoose never thought it was good for berthing babies before. Well now they do.

Something which used to make me sneeze was the smoke from the fire box in my canoe. Every February on the Harrison I used to go fishing for silver spring salmon and it was always at night by torch light. It would be very cold and like all Indians I used a fire box in the canoe and rich fir pitch wood for the fire. So I had this white friend who used to wonder how Indians kept themselves warm on these cold nights and one night he asked me if he could come along with me. Sure I said. I had a very short canoe which meant the fire box would be quite close to him where he sat at the stern. Well we were out on the river for an hour and a half and when we landed all I could see of him in the dark was the whites of his eyes when he blinked. The pitch wood made heavy black smoke and he was blacker then hell and he was also far from being cold. Poor guy. He never did ask me to go fishing again.

I guess I haven't told you any salmon fishing stories yet have I?

Well here's one my stepfather's dad told us kids when we were small. Maybe 300 years ago there were a tribe who lived at Chehalis Lake and there were another tribe about 13 miles up stream from them, north of the present Chehalis Reserve on the Harrison River. And for some reason these two tribes were not on friendly terms so the lower tribe set up fish traps to stop the fishes from reaching Chehalis Lake and hoping to starve out the upper Indians.

They had some fleet-footed braves in those days. They would select one or more of their fastest runners to run down the 13 miles and destroy the traps and then run back home all the same night. They found that a dry salmon sockeye head was the best torch for this purpose. It was rugged country and they could make the 26 mile trip using only one dried salmon head. So they kept the fishes running up the Chehalis most of the time.

There was this Indian and his son I knew from North Vancouver who went up to Rivers Inlet on the coast to fish commercially for Mr. Sockeye. And as you all know every body is inclined to be a little crooked some time. The real trick is always to be a little crooked, not to let it get you so as you make it a habit.

His name was Joe and he made their set with their long salmon net and then he and his boy went to sleep. When they woke up there was another salmon net right beside his with quite a lot of big salmon gilled in it. So he says to his son let's get to work, see all those salmon there, use your knife and don't spare the web, get those fish off quick as possible because we don't want to get caught stealing fish off somebody else's net. Those nets are maybe 250 fathoms long and so the work started. When they reached the other end of the net, throwing off all the fishes in the meantime and stashing them away in their hold, they found out when they came to the end of it by golly, that it was their own net which the tide had made to double back.

While they spent that day mending their net Joe lectured his boy never to steal fish off somebody else's net. Too much work involved. They learned the hard way.

Once I knew a pretty Indian girl from the west coast of Vancouver Island who met a nice young man from the Fraser Valley and they got married. She took her new husband back to her home by the sea to meet his new in-laws. While there he saw hanging up what looked to him like strips of dried salmon and he pulled down a piece and ate it and liked it very much.

Next morning his wife said if you are going to live here you have to learn how to fish, so carrying a basket and a long stick she led him to a meadow with knee high grass. There's one, she says and she clobbered a snake and threw it into the basket. This went on all morning and she killed a lot of snakes.

What's this got to do with salmon her man asks. This is the dried salmon you thought you were eating last night she says. So late that night when she was asleep, he stole a dugout canoe and leaving his pretty bride he paddled all the way down the coast and across the Strait until he came to the mouth of the Fraser river and then he paddled all the way up the river to his old home in the valley. And she never saw him again and I don't blame him.

But I think the salmon story I like best is about the young sockeye that was kidnapped.

When he didn't show up for supper all the other fishes, the coho, the steel-head and the humpback were told about him and the search was on.

But the hump-back is a lazy kind of fish and he said I'm too tired, I will be there tomorrow he said. But he never showed up and he never showed up the next day or the day after. As a matter of fact he never showed up until a whole two years had gone by. And do you know that is why the humpys only come up the Fraser river every second year.

Well, the search is still on for the kidnapped young baby sockeye and that is why the hump's tomorrow is every second year.

So I guess that about finishes the twenties and now I have to start remembering about the Hungry Thirties.

Part 3

I Remember My 1930s Days

Things got damn tough in the '30's. No jobs to be got hardly.

I had a friend Jack, that owned an old car and when he gassed up at a service station he would put only one gallon at a time in for fear that his back tires may blow up on account of the weight. Another friend owned a drug store at the Five Corners at Chilliwack. When I went to visit him one November day he says to me I can't sell any of my medicines, nobody seems to be getting sick. But on the other hand there were a lot of sick people who couldn't afford to buy any medicines.

There were no such things as family allowance, no unemployment insurance, no welfare. You had to be very desperate before you got any relief and it was very limited.

The Government built a lot of relief camps for the single men and they got paid the big sum of 20 cents a day and their board and bed. There were men from all walks of life, university guys, professional workers from all different trades. I knew one guy that looked after the Delco light plant and he got 35 cents a day. Boy was he a big shot. You couldn't hardly touch him with a ten-foot pole.

My children were quite young at the time but I was more fortunate than some. I was very progressive and I always managed to find work of some sort. And of course the work I followed was logging.

In 1930, the year after the Chehalis camp had gone belly up, I found a job in a camp west of Abbotsford up above the valley. It was a steam railroad show, their own saw mill at Mill Lake and they were logging the finest stand of virgin fir timber in the whole country side. Some of the men had worked there for 35 years. Hell if you worked there only 20 years you were just a new man. However I got a job there. It was flat country and none of that tough sledding side hill kind of work, but there was a lot of underbrush and devil club.

Ever see devil club? Stay away because it's murder. It looks like a beautiful plant that grows in a tropical country and is way taller than a man. Its stems are as thick as your wrist with great big leaves. It grows thick together, so thick you would call it impenetrable and its thorns are as long as needles, every inch of it. These needles are so strong they won't break and it will tear a man's flesh to ribbons as well as his clothes, besides giving him a bad rash he won't get over for a long long time. It sure as hell is called by the right name.

Any ways the outfit was going to move their big steam donkey to a new setting and when they were ready to string out the straw line around the first quarter they would go maybe a thousand feet from the donkey. The straw line was in four or five hundred foot sections, I forget. So the hook tender he grabs the $10 end of the straw line and strikes out through the under brush which was way higher than he was and thick like a tropical jungle. After a bit the straw line it unhooks from the rest of the line, or rather when I think of it, the first extension disconnects from the first part of the line he had strung out, and the brush was so thick the poor guy couldn't get turned around and he got lost, which was damn easy to do in that jungle.

Well we didn't see him again for four days and all the time he was dragging this four hundred foot heavy cable. He finally showed up when he broke through to a road near Clearbrook and he was a bloody mess from all the devil club. He still had his cable too.

The company had two steam loco motives and the biggest one was about 25 tons. The loci engineer who we call the hogger had worked there for so long he knew every low joint and every inch of the rail track. And every time the brake man would signal him to stop he would stop. Then he would fall asleep. He was the sleepiest man I ever met up with. Then when the brake man wanted him to move the train ahead or back up he would have to walk all the way up to the loci to wake the engineer up. Then as soon as the train was ready for a haul to the dumping ground and was rolling along nicely, the hogger he would fall asleep again. When he came to the one road crossing he would reach up in his sleep and blow the whistle and then just when he got near to the dump he would wake up for good. Maybe you won't believe this story but it is true. I swear it.

To keep down the food store expenses I would hunt for deer because deer meat is very good and this one nice fall day all I had left in the way of ammunition was one 30.30 bullet. Well I was gone for about an hour when I spotted and killed this good deer clean. As I was packing my deer home I heard my dog barking which I had left at home chained up. He was sounding off directly ahead of me and in a minute came these two deer running towards me down the deer trail I was following.

I laid down my deer and picked up a good sized rock and moved sideways off the trail about four steps. When Mr. Deer came jumping by I let him have it with this rock and I couldn't miss I was so close by. I broke the poor deer's back and so there was my deer number two. Two deer with only one bullet.

When I finally packed both of the deer home and that was a job, my wife doubted my work. Besides it was April Fool's Day. But when I had skinned both of them and she couldn't find no bullet mark on one of them, then she believed me.

My dog that was tied up? Oh he had tugged off his collar

and had taken off to track me down and find me. He was a good tracker that one.

Speaking of One Shots once I heard of this great Indian bear hunter in northern British Columbia who was about 98 years old. All he wanted before he died he said was to have just one more shot at a grizzly bear. And he had two grand sons about 14 years old and 16 years old.

So he asked the two boys to take him to a certain tree he knew way back in the hills. They made a stretcher of poles and an old blanket to carry him in and it was a pretty tough carry for them. Then just as they came up to this certain tree they saw a very big black bear coming along towards them. Sure enough it was Mr. Grizzly. So they dropped the stretcher with their old Grandpa in it and they ran away. They were both crying when they got home and told their mother I guess that's the end of grandpa. So the mother says to the boys stop crying you two, your grandpa got home a half hour ago. Boy he sure must have been a tough old guy.

And I mustn't forget about Fenn and his wife who had these two friends, a couple out of Vancouver, and who came up the valley to see them for a weekend. So the four of them journeyed up to Chehalis Creek where I was spending some time on a job of clearing the creek of a log jam pile that was blocking the channel. They brought along their shot guns because this was in the fall and that's duck time.

While we were chatting about this and that a lonesome old mallard duck came flying down the stream. Well Mrs. Fenn she took aim on the duck but she forgot to pull the trigger until it was too late. Then when she did pull the trigger she over balanced and fell flat on her back on the edge of the creek. Old Mr. Mallard he just quacked a couple a times and kept on winging home for it was getting on his supper time. We all sure had a good laugh about it, all except Mrs. Fenn that is.

You remember about all that logging equipment that was

left to rust away in the bush that I was telling you about in 1929? Well in 1931 I got me the job of moving it all out of the woods down to a beach camp.

Our first job was to rebuild a high wooden trestle of the railroad where a mud slide had pushed half a dozen bents right away from the bridge. And there were all sorts of mud slides and other tough things to contend with. When we got the trestle repaired we started to move the cold deck machines to the camp by loading them on to the cars. Then the super orders us to chop off the skidder lines right where they came off the drums and to leave the lines lying there just strung out into the bush to be salvaged later. Then there were four sky lines to be spooled up. They were 2500 feet long and two and a half inches diameter so that part was quite a chore. So piece by piece we managed to round up everything except 500 feet of two inch water pipes which used to take water to the steam donkey. And when it was all done and all gone to the beach camp and just stashed there I was out of a job again.

Around about this time I was renting a little dwelling for me and the wife and kids from a rancher on the north side of the Harrison river. When I was lucky to get a 25 cents an hour temporary kind of job in the Agassiz area we moved there for a couple of months. I was lucky because there just wasn't anything else at the time.

Well one week end we drove back to the ranch to check on our old house and after we opened the gate we parked the car in the field and we walked maybe a hundred yards to the house which was high, maybe eight steps up to the front door.

I just happen to look out a window and damn if there isn't this big mean looking Jersey bull and he's charging towards the car like a bat out a hell. I beat it out a the house and quick thinking like, I run in a parallel line with him. He spots me, stops, squares off and then starts coming at me.

So far so good because what I had in mind was a little old

log cabin that was close by that had a window about four feet above the ground with no glass in it. That old angry bull was right at my heels when I dived through head first just like a acrobat. Well he sure was in a rage and he even tried to climb the big maple tree that was next to the cabin.

So then my wife she started hollering and imitating a bull from the house and he turned around and started charging off toward her. This gave me the time I needed to get the car out of the field and close the gate. So then it was my turn to bellow like a bull and I ran to a far corner of the field bellowing and the bull he starts coming at me but I was outside the fence and quite safe. That was how my wife and the children got their chance to run to the gate and escape.

I suppose you think all this ruckus was because I didn't want to get my car broken up which was a good enough reason because in those days that old car was real important. But the other reason was because my mother in law and baby infant were in the car as well. It has been over 40 years since it happened and I remember like it was last month.

Just before Christmas in '31 a super arrived at my place from Vancouver and asked me if I would undertake the job of moving all the equipment stashed at the beach camp over to the Vedder River near Chilliwack. Thank you I said, I am damn glad to get the work. Well he says, this time you hire your own crew. And for God's sake he says, don't you go hiring any of those Harrison home brews.[1]

What he meant was some of those rum pots[2] we had on the previous job and that included one certain brake man with a air ticket.[3] Those guys sure shuffled their feet on the job before and that super didn't miss a trick all the time it was going on.

Well I rounded up a good crew pretty quick, all good reliable men and I didn't have to look very far for a donkey engineer as my older brother had a steam certificate.

So the job was going along smooth as duck down and I

had to do some switching with the loci and I took on the job as brake man for awhile which was a job I knew well enough except I didn't have any air ticket. Sure enough this brake man I wouldn't give the job to wired down to Vancouver and reported on me that I was braking without a air ticket. He reported to some train men's union.

The super comes up from Vancouver and the first thing he said to me was well Hank, I hear you don't have a air ticket. Don't let that worry you he says, and he gave me to understand that being foreman of the job I was privileged to do any job I liked. Anyway I had a brake man with a ticket due any day.

A lot of the equipment we shipped by scow to the Vedder. All the rolling stock went by C.P.R. to Mission City and crossed over the Fraser to Abbotsford. Then it went on the B.C. Electric interurban line to the destination.

I had two steam tow boats standing by when ever I needed them and we had the big steam donkey engine loaded on the scow. They both hooked on the scow and started towing it down the river and for some reason I don't know the skipper takes a short cut around a bend and grounds the scow hard. I saw what the score was and went and told the super who just happened to be in camp at the time.

So I got my brother and his little speed boat and the three of us went down to where the hang up was. The super was mad as hell but he didn't say much and he emptied a package of cigarettes in short order. He would light up and take three or four puffs and throw it away and so on and so on.

Finally the other skipper he gets a brain wave and decides he's going to make use of it. He had a good fast engine so he started circling the scow with his boat in order to make swells. Slow at first, his wheel held hard over, he picked up speed gradually getting the feel of the race course. The scow was ninety feet long. As he circled around it as close as he could it wasn't very long before he had her wide open. Boy what a show, and all for free as we stood on the scow watching her zip around and around. The other boat was still pulling for all it was worth and the waves got bigger and bigger. Then the scow started to move. Honest.

Without a word the super glances at me sideways and grins and lights a cigarette only this one he didn't throw away. Those two captains respected that point after that. They stayed in the channel and gave it plenty of room.

The place where we were moving the equipment from had been turned into a Government relief camp[4] some time before and there must have been over a hundred men there. They got 20 cents a day plus board and bed. So while we were working around there we always had a big audience, some times too many, specially when we were switching cars around with the loci. There were four such Government camps like that in that one district alone.

We had a soccer club in Chehalis at the time and we got a lot of good competition from teams made up at the camps. All in all they were a good bunch of soccer players and good sports as well.

I remember one relief guy who saved up a bit of change and went on a drunk. Next morning he had a hangover so he goes to a confectionary store for a ginger ale. He takes a few sips and then whispers to the clerk is this the best you got? The clerk says just a minute and takes the half bottle of ginger ale to the back room and fills it up with plain water. When he brings it back the guy says how much? Oh about a quarter the clerk says. And the guy paid it and went away happy.

Two more I remember were a couple a guys from the camp who asked me for jobs as car knockers. Don't suppose you under-forty types know what that is either, do you? Well in those days and for a long time before, all railroad wheels were made of cast iron not steel like today, and those older kind wheels would some times get a crack in them which could let the wheel break into pieces while the train was running thus causing a bad derailment. And the only way you could tell if a wheel was still sound was by tapping it with a small hammer. It was good if it rang like a bell. It was bad if it clunked. So guys who walked the length of a stalled train with long-handled hammers tapping the car wheels were called car knockers and when they got to each coupling they also inspected those.

In the days of those crack C.P. and C.N. passenger trains that crossed Canada in four days and five nights, car knockers would tap the wheels at every major 20-minute stop over, day or night. Another thing they would do at the same time would be to stuff each wheel bearing with cotton waste soaked in oil and it was a real messy job. But all that kind of thing is long gone now.

Any way, back to those relief guys, I took a chance and put them on the pay roll car knocking and inspecting my made up trains of equipment. Then when they had done the work the C.P.R. inspector made his inspection and their job passed with flying colours. I didn't find out until later they were two university professors. It was men like that too who couldn't get jobs in the Bad '30's.

So all the equipment got set up again at the new location on the Vedder River and by the spring of '32 everything was in operation. There had been another outfit there that had pulled out and all the old bunch moved back again and fitted in real good. I got the job as head loader which at $4.50 for an eight hour day was one of the better paid jobs. Choker men got $2.75 a day and a high rigger got $5.50 a day. And all of them less $1.20 for bed and board. Hell today there's not one of those jobs gets less than $40 a day and better. I was sure born too soon.

Being a new man there I was kinda out of place in the camp. At first I had with me one of the other head loaders who had worked there before, second loading for me, and after a while I had the other one. They were two good guys and good workers. No friction of any sort. And it made my job more simple having two men of good experience working for me.

Just the loading engineer thought it wasn't right me having the job instead of one of the other guys and he made things rough for me. Maybe he thought I didn't have the experience but I kind a think that my being also a half breed had something to do with it. One day he over played his hand. I didn't know the super had been watching him too and in a loud voice so the foreman could hear it too he says to me Hank, do you know where's there a good logging engineer available. If you think of one let me know.

I suppose the foreman told the engineer, anyway I had a changed engineer after that and he knew that I could turn him in any old time. Well things ran pretty damn smooth after that and I guess it wasn't until after that happened that I began to really feel one of the boys for the first time and could relax a little.

There were some of the boys who took their lunch into the bush in a paper bag instead of a bucket like most. And there was this spy in the camp, a hard boiled bob tailed squirrel who would be right there every morning watching where the men stashed away their lunches in the bags. Then during the morning while the guys were working he would raid every bag and he wouldn't just take a bit or two from one or two. He would smash up the works. It was a daily routine for Mr. Squirrel. The guys tried to way lay him but he was too smart. Whenever we moved the steam donkey to a new place he would be there waiting for us. Every day was one big picnic for him. That year when the camp shut down for the winter it was a long and cold one and the next spring he never showed up. I know what happened though, he probably froze or starved to death, probably the latter, because while he was busy robbing the lunches and getting fat on cake and cookies and sandwiches and pies he wasn't storing up fir cones and hazel nuts for the winter. Mr. Squirrel just like some people just never ever learned.

There was no such thing as unemployment insurance then. If you wanted to eat in the winter months you had to save up enough during the summer season and there was if

Agassiz Hop yards.

'I got a job at the Sumas yard and there was about 700 pickers, Indians from all over the country. Some of the elderly ones would start picking at day break and so as to be fair to everybody as there was so many pickers my job was patrolling the fields, keeping the pickers off until seven in the morning. Boy that was the worst job I ever had because it was next to impossible to keep them away from the vines. They'd bawl me out in their own languages and I'll bet my last bale of hay there was seven or eight different Indian languages there. The job was getting me down since with my regular day's work, I was because of the patrolling working 13 hours a day at least. So I bought a bottle of 40% Jamaica rum because that was about the only good thing about being a half breed, I could buy liquor. Not all the time. Just sometimes.' (p. 30)

Hank (bottom row, second from right) on the Chehalis Lacrosse Team at Skwah, ca. 1920.
'What they play now is box lacrosse and that is a lot different from field lacrosse in the old days. We didn't have any pads and helmets and protection like that, not even gloves. The field was the same size as a football field not the little dinky thing they use now, and there were no boards to play a rebound off of. There were twelve men to a side and no extras or substitutes, and what you did you just got out there in the open sun and you ran and ran and ran all the time and if a man got hurt bad that was it.' (p. 26)

Chilliwack Brass Band.

'Did you know that in those days most all the bigger reserves had Indian brass bands? Oh yes. Much later on at the big year-ly exhibition in Vancouver the Indian brass band competitions was something everyone looked forward to. Although none of them was educated too well, they sure could read their music notes, but I myself do not know one note from another.' (p. 9)

Sternwheeler *Beaver*.

'I remember watching the old ... Beaver blowing lots of black smoke and sparks come chugging up the river to the Hatzic Landing.... Then the bigger boys would get into their canoes and paddle out to meet her and get bounced around by the waves and swells the old Beaver made.' (p. 5)

Hank, his wife, Margaret (née Leon), and their daughter Beatrice, ca. 1925.

'And on December 9, 1924, when I was 20, I signed the life long contract for better or for worse. Which meant I really had to work for the rest of my life. Funny part of it all is we were born on the same month, same year, baptized on the same day, got married the same day and we got our first child the same day. And soon. And we didn't go on any honeymoon either.' (p. 30)

Steam Donkey, ca. 1930s.
'Then there was this steam donkey engine which we called a steam pot that
a crew was using to load a car with logs out of the lake. It was an old pot and
while they were working the boiler part blew up. The two loaders took off.
One ran along the shore with his peevee hook in his hand. He stopped and
looked back and he saw the steam still spouting and he just kept on running. The other loader took off for the tall timbers and nobody saw him
again for four days. As for the poor loading engineer who was standing next
to the steam pot when she blew up I never did hear what happened to him.
He maybe still flying around in Heaven for all I know. Anyway he didn't
have to work no more.' (p. 25)

Cold deck. Possibly Hank on the far right, ca. 1935.
'When we got the trestle repaired we started to move the cold deck machines to the camp by loading them on to the cars. Then the super orders us to chop off the skidder lines right where they came off the drums and to leave the lines lying there just strung out into the bush to be salvaged later. Then there were four sky lines to be spooled up. They were 2500 feet long and two and a half inches diameter so that part was quite a chore. So piece by piece we managed to round up everything except 500 feet of two inch water pipes which used to take water to the steam donkey. And when it was all done and all gone to the beach camp and just stashed there I was out of a job again.' (p. 45)

Hayrack boom loading logs onto railcars, Chilliwack River Valley, ca. 1935.

'Then we took Mr. Fir and cut him up into 40 foot lengths and you would get only one length on a rail car. And a stumpy little Shay loci looking like a kindly old St. Bernard dog would hitch on to maybe 50 of those cars and she would beeeep her whistle and waddle them down a twisty narrow gauge rail line through the deep forest to the salt chuck. Her monkey action gear on both sides would flash and her pistons would chug and steam would belch out both her ears and smoke would come out her head and boy that sure was a sight to make a man feel he was doing something big in the world. With the size of the tools we had in those days to do the big job with, it gave guys a feeling of accomplishment that the job was getting done at all.' (p. 60)

Two speed yarder loader, ca. 1940.

'We had a big 12x14 steam unit by this time, for yarding the logs in with and I remember this high ball wood's foreman standing behind the yarder engineer who was running her at three-quarter throttle. The Bull of the Woods finally got so he couldn't stand it any longer and he shouts to the engineer this thing's got only two speeds, wide open or shut. So the engineer sure punished that old yarder after that.' (p. 36)

Hank, as Head Loader, disconnecting log from Hayrack boom onto railcar.
'So all the equipment got set up again at the new location on the Vedder River and by the spring of '32 everything was in operation. There had been another outfit there that had pulled out and all the old bunch moved back again and fitted in real good. I got the job as head loader which at $4.50 for an eight hour day was one of the better paid jobs. Choker men got $2.75 a day and a high rigger got $5.50 a day. And all of them less $1.20 for bed and board. Hell today there's not one of those jobs gets less than $40 a day and better. I was sure born too soon.' (p. 49)

Steam donkey on 'sleigh' using its own power to drag itself to the logging site.

' … [T]he outfit was going to move their big steam donkey to a new setting and when they were ready to string out the straw line around the first quarter they would go maybe a thousand feet from the donkey. The straw line was in four or five hundred foot sections, I forget. So the hook tender he grabs the $10 end of the straw line and strikes out through the under brush which was way higher than he was and thick like a tropical jungle. After a bit the straw line it unhooks from the rest of the line, or rather when I think of it, the first extension disconnects from the first part of the line he had strung out, and the brush was so thick the poor guy couldn't get turned around and he got lost, which was damn easy to do in that jungle. Well we didn't see him again for four days and all the time he was dragging this four hundred foot heavy cable. He finally showed up when he broke through to a road near Clearbrook and he was a bloody mess from all the devil club. He still had his cable too.' (p. 42)

Spar tree surrounded by 'yarded logs' ca. 1935.

'Well a choker man has a tough job for one thing. After a tree is cut down and is just lying there it was his job to poke a hole under the tree so that a big steel cable can be pushed through and then made into a sling. Then the sling is hooked to another big cable attached to the winch that runs off the old steam pot. Then the log is dragged back through the slash to gradually build up a big storage pile at a centre location. The pole that stood up in the middle of this pile that held the sheaves for the pulling cable was called a spar tree.' (p. 33)

Descending a big Douglas Fir spar tree after topping and limbing, 1942.
'That fall I helped out a little, two of my friends who were going to start
a small gypo logging camp outside of Chilliwack by climbing up and topping off a spar tree for them. It was a fine Sunday morning and I had
quite an audience that day. There were hill billies came from all over the
country. It wasn't very high, only about a hundred feet maybe. I went out
a my way to do the job for the guys just for the promise of a day's pay
when they got their operation under way. Which pay I never did get. Of
course I will always have it coming.' (p. 55)

Big Douglas Fir on the back of truck, Bowman Mill, Chilliwack, ca. 1935. Note three Aboriginal men in centre.

'You take a virgin Douglas Fir tree that has spent maybe two hundred, three hundred years to grow arrow straight and maybe two hundred feet high and that is about eight feet through at the butt. In my thinking which I know is old fashioned I think there is some thing dirty about a man now who is able to cut it crashing down in less than a half hour all by himself using a six foot gasoline chain saw. What chance does the poor tree have?' (pp. 59–60)

OTOGRAFTS
LIWACK, B.C.
ANADA,

Cottonwood Corner, Chilliwack (now Hwy 1, exit 119) during flood of 1948.

'I got this call to go to the Compensation Board office for a checkup and wouldn't you know it was the exact time of the highest part of that disastrous flood of '48 in the Fraser Valley.... So the wife and I we crossed the river by canoe and we caught the train into Vancouver. A few miles further the train was delayed on account of injured cattle on the line which had to be shot. There was cattle all over the higher levels that had moved up from the valley by themselves to escape the rising water. The Dewdney army boats were working hard rescuing people. The whole area was one big disaster area.' (pp. 67–8)

Hank and Margaret, 1989.
'The house is more of a cottage, gray asphalt shingle siding, and there's a fair size living room and two bedrooms and a pretty good kitchen with an oil stove and a electric stove, where Margaret, the wife, cans things out of the garden like tomatoes, beans, carrots and corn and which is about the only exercise I get nowadays. And that's where the telephone is, in the kitchen.' (p. 75)

you planned it right always a little bit extra even for a bottle of whiskey every once in a while. Which is what happened all through 1933. Just routine logging six days a week and no time for mischief except the dances on Saturday nights, but most all the time watching every penny for the next winter. I was lucky to be working with so many poor guys not able to at all.

1934 was the year we began to build up our loggers union and all the camp owners didn't help us any. The union organizers had to walk long miles in to every camp and then out again regardless how far a camp was from a rail centre. All the managements gave out strict orders they were never to be picked up or helped although we all wanted to.

I nearly had a nasty accident that year. I had to move a 40 foot railroad car of oil down to the siding and it was half full. I got her going with a wheel wedge kind of lever we used to use and I could stop her with the hand brake. Only trouble was every time I would get the damn thing almost stopped, the oil inside would surge to the front of the tank with such a force, away we'd go again. And you daren't lock a thing like that tight because a skid is worse than ever. Well I finally got her stopped, me riding on top hitting the hand brake, fifty feet to go before I would come to a steep incline and there anything could a happened.

Because this incline was the same one where a friend of mine had been killed only a few days before. He was a brake man and he hooked on to a car load of logs with the Galloping Goose which was the 4 Spot or the small gas loci that had air brakes. It is my guess he didn't put up the retainer on that car which is part of the air brake system and you can fix it for high or low pressure depending on the grade. It is operated from the loci. Without this extra pressure a loci engineer hasn't much of a chance.

So the loci driver couldn't control his heavy load of logs, maybe seven thousand feet of logs. He charged down this same old incline and there was a run a way and a bad smash up and one killed brake man. We had ourselves a bit of a booze up that night.

The next Sunday evening after Saturday night and most of Sunday at home with the wife I caught the 7:15 speeder back to camp with a kind of flat car observation trailer behind, and all the boys were already on it. When we got going they passed me a five gallon can of gasoline only there was wine in it, not gas. There was about 20 miles to travel and by the time the speeder got to camp the wine was almost gone. It sure must have looked funny us all drinking gasoline as we speeded along. Lucky there was no top brass around. So the next morning was sure a blue Monday and quite a number of the gang couldn't even eat their breakfast.

1935 everything was going smooth until the winter came. Boy it was rough. We were living in Chilliwack by then and it was so cold the undertaker friend of mine couldn't bury any dead for two weeks. He had the corpses sitting around all over his place. In the spring of '36 there was a sudden spell of warm air and then it was worse. There were bad floods all over the valley and the old Fraser was still frozen over. When the ice did decide to break up and drift it formed an ice jam at the mouth of the Harrison which caused that river to back up.

Jimmie on the Chehalis Reserve woke up this morning and looked out the window. He couldn't believe what he saw. There were big stumps and trees flowing past his place all drifting the wrong way, up stream. Do you know that back up, wrong way current almost went as far as Harrison Lake and that is a long ways from the Fraser. Then to top it all off we had a silver thaw that followed everything else. All the power poles were down all over the valley and we lived half a mile from town and were without any electricity for two weeks, which was rough because we had all these electric appliances. I suppose you think that is funny because I am Indian sort of.

That reminds me I have not told you about how the Indi-

ans kept warm in the old days. They didn't put on a Cowichan sweater[5] like my wife knits for us all now. They would
make a thin cord from cedar bark which is fine and stringy
and can be used for all sorts of useful things. They then
would use this to hang up a large rock about the size of a
man's head about three feet off the ground. They would
then lie down underneath this rock at night time and just
thinking about what would happen if the fine cord would
break would make them sweat and stay warm all night.

I am not fooling you as my stepfather's dad told us kids
that story and I always believed him.

And he told us another story about the cold. Chief
Johnnie had to go to the Indian Chief's meeting early next
morning and since he had to get up so early to paddle
maybe 20 miles, he decided to stay up all night instead. It
was very cold and he lit a big fire in his stove deciding to
stay by the fire and keep warm. He pulled his rocking chair
up close and he put both his heels on the bar and locked
his hands across his knees. As the fire got hotter the Chief
he fell asleep and his chair rocked back and his legs
straightened out and he scorched both his soles on the
stove. What's the matter with you he yells at the stove as he
wakes up sudden. And he bawled out the stove for five minutes and after that the old stove never did keep him quite
so warm again. I always remember that story when Temptation makes me want to swear at some piece of equipment
that don't do what it is supposed to. Poor innocent stove.

Now that this part of my story is talking about Chilliwack
lately, because this is where we lived about this time, I guess
I better tell you how Chilliwack got its name. It is not a
Indian story and I guess it is pretty bad but some people
laugh when I tell it. Any ways there was this ice peddler on
the Squah Reserve who knocked on the door of an Indian
woman's house and when she said no she didn't want any
ice today, the peddler tried to get smart with her. So she
grabbed his chunk of ice he was carrying and hit the ice
man on the top of the head with it. When he sort of come

to he says, gee lady, that was a chilly whack, so now you know.

There were a lot of strikes in the logging camps around that time mostly because the owners wouldn't recognize the organizers or anything else about a union, and we used to donate a day's pay every so often to the strikers fund. In our opinion we were doing the right thing. But now today, as I sit here and think about it, my opinion is in reverse. They are all going to extremes. And so are all the rest of the different unions. They will soon have to draw the line before they over do it, if they already haven't gone overboard with all their bigger and bigger demands by now. I think it will be a sad thing for the whole country if the organizers don't draw the line pretty damn soon because pretty soon all the owners of all the places supplying the jobs are going to say finally we can't ever pay not one cent more and if you don't take it then we are all just going to close up and go to California and enjoy ourselves. Then there will be no more jobs and then what? I think a lot of those organizers get their big salaries and their cars and their office to sit in strike or not, while the guys which are doing the real work are walking on a picket line most times in the rain. Why won't the union guys ever see that. It is a big mystery to me.

Excuse me when I say all that but I think I got a right to because I was one of the boys and I worked damn hard too. I got a fair day's wages for a good day's work when you think what those times were like. And it was up to us all in those days to make the most we could out of ourselves, not sit around and whine about that wages are so low they can't afford a new car every year or their wife's refrigerator is five years old.

What I think is the real real trouble today is nobody has any ambition anymore to be a better work man than the next guy or to turn out a first class piece of work. I guess those days are over and it is just too damn bad I think.

I also think that they all should a been born half breeds

then they would know how to work hard to make their way and stay ahead and be better than another guy.

That fall I helped out a little, two of my friends who were going to start a small gypo logging camp outside of Chilliwack by climbing up and topping off a spar tree for them. It was a fine Sunday morning and I had quite an audience that day. There were hill billies came from all over the country. It wasn't very high, only about a hundred feet maybe. I went out a my way to do the job for the guys just for the promise of a day's pay when they got their operation under way. Which pay I never did get. Of course I will always have it coming.

The long cold winter of 35–36 with the bad ice jams meant there was a long shut down for us loggers. This was bad news for a bull cook we had in camp from the Old Country. He never drank anything but the very best liquor and he used to make fun of all the rest of us guys that drank cheap liquor such as gin, beer or wine. Well the shut down got hard on his bank book and he had to economize. So he took to drinking gin and beer and by the time the camp opened up again in the late spring this bull cook was a full fledged alcoholic. It was kind a hard on his pride but us common guys understood. Let that be a lesson to all you gin and beer drinkers. Watch out.

While I was waiting for the camp to open I went second-rigging in the Harrison Lake area but there was quite a feud going on between the head rigger who was the foreman, and the hooker, and it wasn't at all good for the company. One of the owners wanted me to take over full charge, but I turned it down. I wasn't going to step in to that hornet's nest of trouble for anything. So, back to my old job at the Vedder. Along about the end of '36 I finally quit the old company and became a bucker and faller for a small camp.

I was 33 years old in 1937 when I went farthest away from the life in the Fraser Valley than I had ever been before. That was the year I finally got out to the really big trees on the west coast of Vancouver Island. I thought I had cut down big trees but those trees near the ocean, boy you almost had to lie on your back to see the top and so big in diameter one butt was the width of a rail car. It was a H.R. MacMillan camp in the Port Alberni area and employed 350 men. It was a good camp and I got the job as head loader, being sent there by the Loggers Agency in Vancouver.

That was the time when all those cowboy songs were popular that my two daughters used to sing and yodel as one of them played the guitar. I came home one weekend from work and our cat he was so glad to see me he jumped into my lap just when the girls were yodelling. So I got an idea that cat could yodel too. I held its four paws and went to work on the small part of its back. When the girls reached a high note or a low note I would squeeze the cat accordingly. Well pretty soon the cat was yodelling like a professional. We never missed a note. Boy we had the bag pipes beat all to hell.

I worked that Alberni camp all through 1938 and a good piece in to 1939 until one piece of the operation was closed down and that let me out as seniority was in effect by then, owing to the unions, and so naturally I was one of those that got laid off. It was about time to leave there anyway because I was getting worried about the places between my toes that were beginning to grow skin like the web of a duck's foot. With all that rain over there it was no wonder.

I arrived back home in the valley just before the damn war broke out. I was thinking about seeing if I could get in to the Army like my brother had done in the First War but just as Luck would have it the Loggers Agency called to tell me that inside of ten days they wanted me to ship out to Ramsey Arm, which was a camp about 135 miles up the coast from Vancouver.

Up there I never will forget this hunch backed cocky little whistle punk which my partner and I thought we could make a great boxer out of.

We had to watch his diet closely as he was a heavy eater, and he was death against the road work part of his training that we worked out for him. We worked him out pretty damn good until this one evening when we had to help the donkey engineer with some overtime work and we were nine miles out of camp. At the same time, the speeder and the loci were in camp, both out of order. After the work was done we phoned camp and ordered up the speeder or the loci and then we found out we would have to walk it out. We got back to camp at midnight and that nine mile hike exactly fitted in to our road work program. He was sure in good shape, and the only trouble was we over trained him and he got hard to handle and he turned on us.

The weather got very hot and the woods got so tinder dry we had to shut down for a few weeks and we all went home. When the weather man thought we had enough rest he caused the weather to change and we were called back to camp. But the over trained whistle punk never did show up again so he probably made the high lights.

So that is the end of the Thirties for me and just as the bad war is starting.

Part 4
I Remember My 1940s and
1950s Days

I folded up my umbrella for good in 1939 at the end of the season on the west coast and came back here to the Harrison district which I haven't left since. So in 1940 I started with the Canadian Forest Products at Harrison Mills and for the next 19 years until 1959 I worked my logging trade in all kinds of jobs. You name it and I done it. And as I think about it now if I was the same age again and you gave me a choice of what I wanted to work at the rest of my life I think I would still want to be a logger.

I was talking to some of my friends about this in the past little while, most of them Indians, and they all think the same as me, and we came to thinking that most likely it is because of lots of things. Like the outdoor life, the work is never always the same like say in a factory, because of the seasons there is some time for fun like hunting and things like that, and most specially it is because it is a man's work and is risky. This last reason is the best one I think because it means an Indian can feel as good as the next guy and from what we see of a lot of whites these days, maybe even better than the next guy.

So with me as a half breed which is neither one or the other, that reason is I guess the best of all.

Anyway us coast Indians make damn good loggers because for all the reasons like I said they put in an extra effort. I have seen whites who shuffle their feet when it's raining hard and find all sort of excuses when all the conditions aren't just right while the Indians just go out there and slog away and get the job done.

The logging business can mean a really good life and good pay for an Indian who wants to spend his life at it and it always is a mystery to me why more of them don't see this. Hell it never hurt me any, except my hips that is, but that is the risk a man has to take and I am not grumbling.

So like I told you I was never without work and some money coming in all through those Depression Days because logging gave me my chance and I was obliged to give it back something in return which was the best effort I could make. Then right after that it was called what they said was a vital industry during the war time which I believe it was, so for me there was no let up in the work I could get.

Of course in those days, which wasn't that long ago, only 25 years, it was a lot more manual labour than it is now.

Which reminds me. I was in Vancouver a couple a years ago just when the annual Loggers Convention was being held at the Bayshore Hotel and the whole great big parking lot was full with a giant collection of the newest designs in logging equipment. I bet every one of them monsters can do the work of twenty men and more each, but also I bet that the men who sit in those nice warm glassed in cabs and move all those pedals and levers and throttles need engineer's papers from some university to run them. Where's the fun? Where's the challenge? Where's the chance for a guy to get in there into the jungle with just his muscle and his brains and slug it out with a tough opponent? I left that show on the parking lot wondering if the guys who operate them things really feel they did a good day's work today. I suppose they do though because sorry for them, they just don't know any better and how could they?

Boy it was sure different in my day.

You take a virgin Douglas Fir tree that has spent maybe two hundred, three hundred years to grow arrow straight and maybe two hundred feet high and that is about eight feet through at the butt. In my thinking which I know is old fashioned I think there is some thing dirty about a man now who is able to cut it crashing down in less than a half hour all by himself using a six foot gasoline chain saw. What chance does the poor tree have?

In my time it took two men at each end of a 10 foot cross-cut saw bucking away for most of a day before old Mr. Fir would give up the ghost. We always knew who was going to win but at least we gave him the chance of putting up a fight for it. And some times in spite he would flip his butt[1] as he died and take a man with him. Yes sir we had respect for Mr. Fir tree but I can't see how a logger can have much respect anymore with all these powerful modern tools to his hand.

Then we took Mr. Fir and cut him up into 40 foot lengths and you would get only one length on a rail car. And a stumpy little Shay loci looking like a kindly old St. Bernard dog would hitch on to maybe 50 of those cars and she would beeeep her whistle and waddle them down a twisty narrow gauge rail line through the deep forest to the salt chuck. Her monkey action gear on both sides would flash and her pistons would chug and steam would belch out both her ears and smoke would come out her head and boy that sure was a sight to make a man feel he was doing something big in the world. With the size of the tools we had in those days to do the big job with, it gave guys a feeling of accomplishment that the job was getting done at all.

So now today seems like a man doesn't need any more muscle strength. Those big 100 ton diesel trucks move in and take not just one butt. They take three and more butts and where's the steam when they drive away? Where's the picture to stir up a man when they zoom down those great logging roads at 40 miles an hour all radio controlled so the uphill empties can get off the road into planned out wide spaces before the downhiller goes by. I understand that up in the Queen Charlottes if one of them really big shows is to prove out economical they have to put at least 30 and more diesel loads into the chuck every day.

I dunno. I can understand that there has to be improvements in everything and that the unions have forced up the price of labour so high engineers have always got to keep finding better ways of doing things with bigger and bigger and better and better machinery and they call it efficiency. I guess it is and I guess they have to, but where's the dignity in it anymore where a man can feel like he's standing ten feet tall?

That's the part I worry about. I know all the young bucks who might read this are laughing at me but also I know that most old timers are agreeing with me.

But I guess I should get back to my story.

There is always something to take the joy out of life and I lost my eldest daughter in death in 1943. Otherwise the time went on just routine with the trees to cut down and haul out and get dumped into the chuck at the booming ground. I was 40 years old by now and as I sit here and try to recall some good stories for you that happened around those years and fellas that I knew, I can't seem to remember anything or anybody worth mentioning. Now why is that I say to myself just now. And after I think about that a while I have decided it is because that when you are young you are more like a sponge with everything you see and everybody you meet and those kind of memories stay inside a person forever. Then when a guy gets older most all that happens is kind of the second time around for him and the memory of it is blurry if he can remember it at all.

But one thing did happen in 1944 which I will always remember and that was when I got jammed between two big logs and injured my hips. The cause was a green horn engineer who was always trying to monkey wrench. I should a kicked his behind off the job long before it happened and it might have better for all concerned, but I was trying to help him hold on to his job. Anyway I had to go on compensation for a spell.

It was spring of the next year before I got back to work as a hooker and a loader, only this time dammit but I found I was also running a regular logging school on the side. I got all the men to break in, all types, even the prairie chickens. There were lots of them that were absolutely hopeless but there were a lot who showed up as being good men and any like that were moved away from me in to higher up training and then I would get more new guys to show the ropes to. I never did get ahead with any of them. They would say to me Hank, you find out if the guy is any good or not. You tell us first.

And of course we were in the middle of war time. There were these big posters all over the place even in the wash rooms and the cook house. All of them had pictures of big tough loggers doing some kind of logging work and the words in great big letters said YOU'RE AT WAR TOO or something like that. So I guess that makes all us loggers veterans too but without the veterans' benefits that is. I guess the governments forget awful easy.

Come the first of July, 1945, there was to be a four day holiday and the foreman called me up during that time to ask me if I would go back to camp right away and clear up the loading of some logs at a landing which wasn't my usual place to work. I high tailed up there on July 4 and that day I almost met my waterloo. I injured my hips again and busted a leg, an ambulance case.

I went back on compensation again for another long time meanwhile taking therapy treatments and for some unknown reason I had a lot of trouble in getting my compensation cheques. My doctor kept sending his progress reports but no cheques came back in return. Finally my doctor referred me to a specialist in Vancouver and after he examined me he picked up his telephone and says to the Compensation Board, now see here, you give this work man his back pay and hurry up about it. Well I got my cheque in pretty damn short order and it came to over $900.

It was late spring, 1946, when my therapy stopped and so did the compensation and I began life with a permanent limp. So I packed up the family and we all went down to Conway in Washington state to pick strawberries. There was maybe 500 Indian pickers in that one camp alone, as well as one hell of a lot Mexicans that work their way all the way up the coast following the spring growing season doing what they call stoop labour. First time I ever saw a gang of trouble shooters in a harvest field. If one berry rancher got behind all he had to do was ring up the trouble shooter boss and almost before he could put the phone down there would be truck loads of extra pickers at work. As the berries ripen very quickly, it was a very good system.

Johnnie was a pal of mine and he met some of these Mexicans. Hi Senior one of them said to him. Johnnie says, I seen yours first. And from then on they became good friends. Another friend from Lillooet learned some Mex words and after that he travelled with them for a while. Being as how he was dark skinned like the Mexicans he had himself a hell of a time going in to all the taverns. He even wore a sombrero and it sure was astonishing how much Mexican he looked.

Because just like in British Columbia, the Washington state Indians were not allowed their liquor either so they all put it up to me to get it for them, where in every case I had to produce my liquor permit.

There was one guy who left a bottle of rye whiskey with me to keep for him and apparently he must have told his brother about it. Late one night when we were all in bed his brother came and demanded the bottle. I told him straight that I couldn't do because it belonged to his brother. You would have thought he would have gone away but do you know what that buggar did? He pulled out a big 38 calibre revolver and started spinning it around his trigger finger like some guy in a western movie.

My wife she whispers to me, Hank it's about time you did something. Sure I says, what? Oh give him a drink she says.

So I gave him a drink out a my bottle and it worked to some extent because he came a little closer but not quite close enough. Lucky for me I used to read a lot of those bang bang stories of cow boys and such and from all that I had learned by reading I was able to seize him up as a amateur. When a right handed amateur pulls a trigger the gun will always swing to the right. Did you ever know that before? It is a very useful thing to know about.

I got out of bed very slowly working on his nerves and while he was still twirling the gun I got to sit on the edge of the bed and I said something to him which brought him a step closer. My plan was working. I said something again and that was it. He came one step closer and I lashed out and hit his hand to the right quickly. When he pulled the trigger he missed me by a hair. I had him by his right wrist quicker than it takes to tell you about it. With some help from the wife and my daughter I had the gun in no time.

So I kicked him out of the shack. Well I couldn't very well kick him as I was hurting from my damn legs. Anyways he ran to his brother's and told every body an old broken down guy knocked hell out a me, and his brother laughed at him and told him he'd learn some day. But I knew he wouldn't because that kind never does.

Next morning the nosy neighbours asked what the shot was all about. I told them the car back fired, and the brother came and took away his rye. I found out then that sure as hell God wasn't mad at me. He must have been with me in order for the buggar to miss me.

Then something else happened a couple a mornings later just as I was getting out of bed. The shack was shaking and every thing was rattling away so bad I thought sure it was from all the drinking the night before. But I looked out the window and the berry pickers were screaming and hanging on to each other. You would have thought it was the end of the world. I almost swore off drinking there and then and I did until I found out later it was a small earth quake that lasted for two minutes.

It was on this Washington trip that I met a old timer about 95 years old. He had been a husky man in his day and was no slouch yet. While we were there he went to see a eye doctor and the doctor gives him glasses to try on. No good he says and he gives him eight or nine more pairs to try on and they were all no good. By this time the optician was getting kind a impatient so he gives the old man a pair of just rims, no glass at all in them. Boy o boy the old man says, great, just the ones. I can see real good through these.

That was also the time I heard about this crew which was slashing and clearing the boundary line between Canada and the United State where it separates British Columbia and Washington, not too far from Chilliwack as it happened. One guy had a lot of money in his money belt and his partner knew about it. So the guy buried his belt somewhere around the slash camp and his partner murdered him but could not find the money. So the white man who told me this story went to a fortune teller in Seattle and he pin pointed right where the money was. So the white man went back to the old camp site to find it and he was frightened away by an apperition or ghost. The Seattle guy had told him he would never get the money because it was not meant for him, but he went anyway.

Well toward the end of '46 I took up a little house in Vancouver and just to get back in to some kind of working shape again I took a job at a salmon cannery in Steveston on Lulu Island in the mouth of the Fraser. It used to be all Japanese country before the war but when the Japs were moved away from the coast after 1941 all the canneries and other places and their fish boats were taken over by the whites.

Then in '47 I went back to logging again thinking about myself that I was Limpy the Logger but I never let anybody else know that to this day, even my family.

There was a new foreman and for some reason he didn't like my looks and I liked him much less. Well this one morning he really showed his authority.

There came a morning when I was talking to him on the platform and he was all smiles. He waited until I was in the crummy, which is our name for the bus which takes loggers out to their jobs in the bush from camp, and he hollers out Hank, we won't need you for a few days. And in front of all the guys. Well in loggers' talk that meant I got the axe.

Couple a days later I became head loader of another camp and there I stayed for the rest of the year. It wasn't a bad outfit until a certain high rigger arrived in the camp.

The way it was was this. The camp foreman was the rigger and slow? boy he could take a two hour job and turn it into all afternoon just like that. So one day I said to the boss if you keep this rigger any longer our pay cheques aren't going to be any good pretty soon. The boss still thought he was a good man and kept him on but things went from bad to worse. Finally I say, boss if that rigger is still here Monday morning I won't be. This camp is too small and there is no room for the two of us.

Come Monday the rigger was gone and good riddance because he was just a nut in a cogwheel.[2] So another rigger shows up and right away it looked like he was on a percentage basis. First thing he did was to lay off my loading engineer who was a guy who really knew his job. I come to work that morning and here's this new loading engineer and I say where's Jimmie? Oh the rigger says to me, we're making some changes around here. That's just fine I says, I'll go and get my time. No, no, no, he says, you stay we need you here.

It soon began to look like he was going to run a skeleton crew. Why do you know he even had his wife working as a whistle punk? And that was rough on the boys because since they didn't know her at all they couldn't swear around like they were used to. They had to swear under their breath and things start boiling up inside a man when he can't let out a good swear when he feels like it.

I didn't like any part of the new arrangement but I was waiting for the right moment. Finally the crew got so small

I knew the time had come to hurt him good so I quit him cold there and then. And I haven't seen him since.

I think it was the week after when a logger neighbour had a birthday and one of his pals came to have a drink with him. And after a while the birthday kid passes out on the lawn outside. So his friend found a couple a boards and made a cross as you would find in a cemetery. And he put on the cross, Here Lies the Remains of Our Beloved Louie Paper Whom Has Passed Away. Then he stuck it in at the guy's head and leaned it forward a little. When he finally comes to boy he really thought he had had it and he went stone cold sober for over a year.

By this time the camp where I had got the axe had a new woods foreman so I went back there as a hooker and loader and of course I was no stranger there. Then of all the bad luck damn if I didn't have another loading accident and my left knee cap got cracked. The doctor cut off my knee cap entirely and I was in the hospital for a long time. When I got out I had to visit the doctor every two weeks and as it turned out later, instead of the doctor sending in my progress report on the proper form, he was sending it by an ordinary letter.

The Board asked me what was going on and when I told them, they had their own doctor see me. He said, if your doctor doesn't want to look after you proper, we will, which was just the opposite of the way it was the first time. So you never can tell.

Then I got this call to go to the Compensation Board office for a checkup and wouldn't you know it was the exact time of the highest part of that disastrous flood of '48[3] in the Fraser Valley.

There was a wash out on the C.P.R. near Agassiz but there was a train still operating from just beyond the wash out back and forth to Vancouver. The Lougheed highway was open as far as Dewdney and all of Nicomen Island in the river was awash.

So the wife and I we crossed the river by canoe and we

caught the train into Vancouver. A few miles further the train was delayed on account of injured cattle on the line which had to be shot. There was cattle all over the higher levels that had moved up from the valley by themselves to escape the rising water. The Dewdney army boats were working hard rescuing people. The whole area was one big disaster area. Well at Dewdney the highway and the C.P.R. run along beside each other and lucky for us a guy driving a truck west along the highway, about Hatzic, noticed the train tracks were starting to wash out. And he flagged down the train in time. A few minutes after that the tracks ahead of the train washed out into Hatzic Lake, highway and all.

So the train backed up again to Dewdney and from there we hitched a ride with two Vancouver Province newspaper reporters on a round about way, way around the head of the lake. We couldn't make any time because the farm road was cluttered with cattle and it was fast getting thinner because the lake was filling up fast. We came to a little store way up in the hills back of Mission where the reporters found a phone to call in their story and from there we could see right over to Abbotsford across the river and it was all water in between. We could see that the south end of the Fraser bridge at Mission had gone down and it looked like the whole dike system had collapsed. It was one big awful mess. So me with my hips and my busted knee walked with the others all the way into Mission because it was safer than with the old car. And that is where I saw the Red Cross in action for the first time. Boy those kind people really get out and do a big job.

And from there we caught a bus to Vancouver where we spent a week after my checkup. And when it came time to go home I hitchhiked a ride with the Canadian Forest Products company sea plane which was the first time for me in a air plane. All in all it sure was some experience.

Towards the end of that year I had to move back to Vancouver to be close to my knee's therapy treatments and that stay ran into 1949. With the help of the Compensation

Board I took a course in saw filing and was able to qualify in the trade. And when I was done there I went back to the Steveston cannery to get enough work to get mobile again before I could go back to the bush.

When I got back to the valley again it was spring and I was just home when a camp operator dropped by and asked me to be the saw filer at his camp. I was leary about it but figuring I had to start somewhere, started in. Everybody seemed satisfied with my filing and I kept on doing that job for quite a spell, until another of my dooms days happened when the first powered chain saw arrived at the camp. So it was goodbye Hank, that was the end of my saw filing career. I quit.

I was out of work for one day.

In the big camp where I had worked previously, I got a job as an auger man down at the booming grounds. That was in 1951 and there I stayed until I quit forever in 1959. I guess it was until that day about the only job I had never worked at before in the logging business. It was a job a man with bad hips and no knee to speak of could do pretty well and it didn't need the same kind of jumping about that is needed back in the bush.

But first I got to remember there might be a lot of people reading this who won't have the slightest idea of any of what I'm going to tell you about now so I better take time out to explain.

Usually saw mills are in one place like in an area where there is a lot of people, and the trees are some place else like way up the coast of British Columbia. And the big question was how do you get the big logs to the saw mill. You float them in booms – at least in my day you floated them.

A boom of logs was usually 66 feet wide by about 18 sections long and a section was about 66 feet also. Depending on what kind of timber the boom was made up of and estimating at today's average price of about $90 to $95 a thousand board feet, an 18 section boom was worth maybe $40,000 at the mill and contained about 450,000 board feet.

Little dinky tow boats with 200 to 300 horsepower engines and crews of two or three, would tow the booms, sometimes taking as long as three months to make a tow from the Queen Charlotte Islands down to a mill in the Fraser River, about 550 miles trip.

Now today all that is fast disappearing. Flat booms like what I have described are used when the tow is no longer than maybe 150 miles. And in their place and from what they tell me, the B.C. coast is the only place in the world where they are used, are the giant-size self loading, self dumping barges that cost maybe three million dollars each. They are almost 400 feet long and about 75 feet wide, the size of a football field. They take a 10,000 ton load which is about two to three million board feet of logs and that's worth about $270,000 at the mill.

They carry their own huge cranes and at the booming ground where the logs are gathered in the water after being felled, the cranes load the logs crosswise on their barge until they are all piled up to the height of a five storey building. They don't even have to be cabled down. Then towed at the end of a 2½ inch steel cable, by a 3000 to 4000 horsepower giant of a towboat that's worth another three million dollars and carries a crew of 10, such a barge makes the trip down from the Charlottes in five days.

So that is quite a difference but it sure takes a lot a money doesn't it?

Then when the barge gets to the saw mill storage area all they do is open the valves on the port side and the sea rushes in to the port tanks and slowly she starts to lean over. When she is leaning well over so that her portside deck is awash, suddenly the logs let go and with a whoosh and a great splash they all dive into the water. It is something you won't forget in a hurry to see and to hear such a sight. Then the barge rebounds out of the water almost like a rubber ball, waddles from side to side a couple a times and finally floats high and free and looking glad it has got rid of a great weight. Within an hour or two she is on the end of her tow line again headed north for another load.

Now the reason for all this, outside of speed, of course, is the teredo salt water boring worm and also the loss of logs in stormy waters. That teredo is one hell of a destructive pest. He's about thick as a pencil and up to a foot long and he has tiny teeth that chomp their way through fresh wood in salt water. He hardly ever goes through the bark from the side. He starts at one cut end and never stops until he comes out the other end, maybe sixty feet away. Then he starts going zig zag back the way he came and by the time he is through that there log looks like a collander you strain vegetables through. It is absolutely good for nothing. So when it was customary to tow logs in flat booms, in the water for months at a time, boy did Mr. Teredo get fat and healthy and what he cost in terms of dollars lost was they tell me gigantic.

Then the last reason, stormy weather, is sort of where I came in as an auger man.

In a flat boom made up of sections, all the logs floated end ways to the tow, and side by side, free. They were corralled by a chain of boom logs, only we called them boom sticks. These sticks were all about 66 feet long and at each end there would be a hole bored through a bout four inches diameter. Then we would take boom chains made up of the best steel with six-inch links about, and chain all these sticks, end to end.

So now you take an 18 section boom. That meant it would need 18 boom sticks on each side, plus two end boom sticks, plus sixteen more sticks running crosswise, called swifters. That totals 54 sticks, all about 66 feet, and each stick has two holes, so that's 108 holes to be augered. And that was my job.

It was a good system and it worked for years except that in storms the waves would start the logs bobbing up and down and the free logs inside would go down while the boom sticks would go up and first thing you knew a log going up would meet a boom log coming down and the boom chain would snap, the bag would open and there went $40,000 worth of logs scattered all over the coast and to hell and gone besides.

So now you know.

Of course I had bored sticks with a hand auger before, now and then, but by the time I took it up as a trade there was this new power auger I had never seen before. As luck would have it on my first day on the job they had just finished altering some parts and wanted me to test it out. They were asking me a lot of questions, hey Hank, what do you think of this, hey Hank what do you think we should do about that, and hell I didn't know sweet fanny adams. So they said you try it out first Hank and they put this big stick under it and stood way back in the clear. With my bum legs and my cane I sure wasn't going anywhere if anything happened.

So I turn on the gas engine and away we go and boy those chips flew in all directions like no augering I'd ever seen before. Well I guess I had too heavy a hand on the throttle but damn if the great big 4 inch drill didn't snap off at the shank and the pieces went flying like bullets for yards and yards and stuck into the walls of the boom shack. The guys all dived in to the water and the first guy who surfaces says Hank that damn thing's dangerous. But nobody got hurt least of all me.

So we put all our heads together and we decided that if we put this bigger fly wheel against the smaller pulley on the motor it would slow her down. So we did and it worked and I used that there machine for one hell of a long time. And I sure thanked the Lord that night for giving me a good strong heart.

Well like I said, that was 1951 when I started boring these holes. Wish I knew how many holes I bored in eight years until 1959. Boy if I had a dollar for every hole I bored I'd be a rich man living in Fiji with six young maidens and a case of Cutty Sark a week.

And that's all I did, me who was high rigger and faller and foreman and head loader and you name it, nothing but holes, holes, holes, holes, holes, holes. I almost went nuts.

Boy but I was slowing down though and I fell in to the chuck[4] quite a bit but of course you weren't a boom man if you didn't fall in once in a while. And it wasn't necessary to wear a life vest like it is now, either. Nor a hard hat. Kid stuff.

Well my legs they weren't helping any and my knee thing was developing the old rheumatiz and then just before quitting time this certain day I was standing on a log in my caulked boots only we call them cork boots and I was leaning across some water pulling another stick in to me with a pike pole, when the pole slipped and in turning quick I banged up my face on a standing stick.

Next morning the super was down at the booming grounds waiting for me. He was concerned about me and he offered me another job as a shovel operator on the railroad right of way. And it wasn't a steam shovel either. It was one of them long handled single spade varieties, for filling pot holes with. I agreed. I said I'd give it a try for awhile because I knew it was either that or nothing in the shape I was in.

But finally after ten days I couldn't stand the job or stand myself any longer. What the hell was I Hank Pennier doing shovelling a shovel for god's sake!

So I quit for good. It was December 23, 1959 when I stopped work for good. I was 55 years old and by damn I was still a young man but like the kids say now, I couldn't cut the mustard any more.

Funny thing was if you remember, my first job in 1920 was wheeling sawdust at a mill, where I used a big scoop shovel, and I ended 39 years later on the end of another kind of shovel.

And what did I have to show for it all? Some broken bones, some eating money, some drinking money, a good family of course, knowing a hell of a lot of good men, having a hell of a lot of fun and the thing inside that a man lives with that tells him when he has done his best with what he had to do it with.

But there were no more pats on the back from the brass and the supers. I was a thing of the past. Progress in the business had taken on right after the war and I was being phased out anyway.

So maybe it was just as well.

Part 5
I Remember the Now Days

So now it is 1972 and 13 years have gone by and I am 68 years old but I am not an old man yet by a damn sight, although with only the little bit I can get around I sure as hell act like one.

Since 1965 home has been this little rented place of an acre size in the corner of the 50 acre dairy farm that used to be the old George Ashby place on the Nicomen Trunk Road east of Mission City. If you ever drive out this way I am easy to find, right on the road and right beside the slough where the road turns sharp north. There are some big cedars and a lonely old pine beside the house and the beat up '62 Galaxie sits out side looking pretty sad.

The house is more of a cottage, gray asphalt shingle siding, and there's a fair size living room and two bedrooms and a pretty good kitchen with an oil stove and a electric stove, where Margaret, the wife, cans things out of the garden like tomatoes, beans, carrots and corn and which is about the only exercise I get nowadays. And that's where the telephone is, in the kitchen.

The big window in the living room has my big chair and a table beside it where I done all this writing. Across the room is the chesterfield and in the corner is the TV where we are pretty lucky to get all the three American network stations in Seattle, the one at Bellingham near the border, and the two Vancouver stations. I like good shootup detective movies and western movies the best but in the westerns with all those Indians which always get the worst of things and always get shot up, I can't put any faith. It's all pretty phoney because Indians were a lot smarter than that and they still are for that matter. And then I have a subscription to Reader's Digest. We don't get any newspapers because they cost too much now but I keep up with the news because of the TV. And the view out the window and across the fields is Sumas Mountain that I know is across the other side of the Fraser River from here but I can't see the old river from my place.

In 1964 the wife and I took over Benny and Dean to bring up as wards. They are two nice Indian brothers, teenagers now, whose family we knew, and they are a big help to us around the place.

You will wonder how we make out, me not working like I used to. Well there's just three ways. There is a little Workman's Compensation, there's the beautiful Cowichan sweaters my wife knits from the wool she cards herself and which she picks herself right off a sheep farm down the way a piece, as well as the prize-winning Salish wool rugs she looms, and some harvest work on some farms around here and after that, mostly, it is welfare – the cheque that comes in the mail every month from the office at Mission.

How do I feel about that? me who was always independent and worked hard as I could for what I earned? And was never without work for 39 years? Not very good but what else can I do about it now? I see all this talk on TV the past couple a years about all the Indians on welfare and I think by golly, that's me they are talking about too. Think Hank I say to myself. Maybe you earned the right better than some others I say, and if it wasn't for all the accidents you had could be you would still be working and pulling your weight. One thing I learned never to do which is never to lie to yourself and so I know I would be still in there pitching away. Maybe it wouldn't be so active a life as it was in the old days, but I know it would be useful and it would be worth the money that now the welfare is providing.

It was thoughts like this that drove me near crazy the first five or six years after I hung up my shovel in '59. I found that it takes a man one hell of a long time to accept the fates but that no matter how hard you fight it there comes a time when you just learn to accept it all and stop fighting.

So that is how I live now and the way it has been since. I just go on from day to day living from day to day and I watch the seasons pass across my window, the rain, the field flowers, the grass blowing, the dry stubble, the snow flakes some times, and one day follows the next day and the wife looks after me good and the kids run in and out and sometimes an old logger friend drops by to have a drink with me and we get in the car and go to Vancouver for a day but we never stay over, about five times a year, and I think of being a altar boy, and my grandfather's stories, and the days in the woods with the big trees, and some of the girls I used to know but I never told you about those did I? because I am a gentleman, and how the brass always used to say Hank that was a good job.

Hey Hank that's enough about all that. You sound like a old man which I am certainly not.

Instead I will tell you about my disease.

I caught it from a friend about ten years ago and it's contagious as hell. It doesn't show up like a rash or pimples, I guess it is more of a fever. I went to a doctor for it and he gave me some pills but they only work in the day time. Night time comes and the thing comes back bad as ever. And it is all over the valley. People 60 and 70 miles a way have it. My wife she has it. Maybe she got it from me. I tell you it is one fierce disease. The name for it is Bingo. Maybe you heard of it.

Bingo bingo bingo. It seems it is the only excitement I got left in life now which is sure some commentary on how life is changed for me, but it gets me out a the house a couple a times a week and you sure get to meet a lot of new faces and old faces that way.

I was always a betting man betting on any thing. Of course there was Two Card Pete, and poker and twenty-one but then there were things like which ant would get to the sugar first and which raindrop would get to the bottom first and which finger would I hold out first and there would always be the big bets at world series time. When I was working with my big auger on the booming grounds the bets would be a couple of cases of beer. And I was pretty lucky. But not with this damn bingo. No sir.

I used to play only one card at first and now I play four cards, and when the disease hits me real hard I play six. There is a consolation because some people play 12 cards at once so they must have the incurable kind. The money I spend doesn't worry me that much and when I go broke I borrow a couple a bucks here and there. What costs a lot though are those damn pills the doctor gives me to cure it.

One thing I learned while playing is to talk to myself because it helps. Of course Hank I say, it's not your fault, it's the caller's fault. He couldn't read off the right numbers if they were four feet high and lit up with lights.

It's sure frustrating when all you need is one certain number to bingo and some lucky guy next to you gets it and hollers bingo and you have to start all over again and so on for the next two hours. Nothing helps. I have changed my shirt, put on clean socks, even took a bath, but nothing seems to make any difference. But maybe the problem is solved. I met a friend who says I should wear a blue shirt while playing. He says it always works for him. You can't lose he says, all gamblers wear blue shirts while gambling. Well if I can raise the money I'll have to buy me a blue shirt. Money is hard to come by but for bingo, that's different.

I will tell you about what a typical bingo night is like.

You drive up to the hall and there are hundreds of cars around it parked every which way all driven by bingo diseased people who come from as far as 80 miles away. You go to the wicket to buy your tickets and you know the man behind the counter pretty good and you say well tonight's the night, and you walk in and there are a lot of your friends.

Someone slaps you on the shoulder, well lucky he says, are you going to win tonight? I am much hoping to you say. Most places you are allowed to select your own cards and you take them and sit down and you start sorting out your favourite numbers on the cards.

Oh before I go any farther here are some good tips. You got to have a rabbit's foot, a wish bone, some old coins and the older the better, a couple a rusty stove bolts and they got to be rusty, a salt shaker and a horse shoe. A horse shoe is specially important.

And one more thing, never use an umbrella to a bingo game even if it's raining real hard. That one sure is bad bad luck.

There are some variations at the different games. At one place the caller will call out, all those who have had a birthday inside the last two weeks stand up and get a free card. Some people have two or three birthdays a year and that is why some people around these parts are aging so fast.

Other games have what we call a Little Joe. The caller draws a ticket from a barrel and the holder of the matching ticket calls out his favourite number from 1 to 75. Then every time that number gets called, that guy gets an extra 50 cents.

People of all descriptions play bingo, Catholic, Protestants and what have you. And so now the game gets going. The caller starts calling and he calls maybe six or eight numbers before he calls your first one. Every body happeee? he says and then a Little Joe number is called and 15 or 20 people call out Little Joe.

Then somebody hollers bingo and everybody else says a prayer under their breath you will most certainly not find in a prayer book. Next game starts and as soon as he calls the first number somebody yells you rat or something else not so polite. Apparently that was the number he needed to Bingo the game before. The caller is called so many bad names it is a good thing he does not hear most of them.

Game over you ask a friend how he made out. Well he says, the caller must have made a mistake because I finally won one. On our way home my wife says I'm through. I am definitely through with bingo. I quit, you hear me Hank, I quit.

Well she misses two or three times, long enough to figure maybe her luck has changed, and she goes back for more, until the next time.

If you don't win at bingo it is because you are likely drinking the wrong brand or maybe going to the wrong church and maybe you are living too clean a life. And it is a good thing you can't get your bingo cards on credit. I hope they keep it that way. Because then I would be in hock the rest of my life. Right now I am just a little bit in hock.

Well whenever I lose at bingo to get over my bad mood I send Benny out in to the garden to weed and tend the vegetables. Work is a good cure. I mind the day Benny came in and said he was working but the shovel hadn't done any work for some time, that it was soft and got tired very easily. Benny is fond of work and he never gets tired himself but he thought it would be better if he gave his shovel a rest every ten minutes until the shovel toughened up a bit. He said when it got its muscle developed then he would really put the shovel to work. The wife was quite pleased with him that evening for all the work he had done but the lazy old shovel hasn't done a thing since and it is now a month later.

Couple a months ago I was in the garden with Benny and we were spading and planting and our cat Little Hobo was sitting on the window sill in the sun just watching us. After we come in to the house I looked out the window and there was Little Hobo working digging a hole in the garden and he planted some thing I don't know what and he covered it up with earth. The weather was just right for planting and I thought well, it remains to be seen whether Little Hobo's garden will grow up or not.

Two and half weeks later, the weather man must have got his wires crossed because there was no rain all that time and the poor cat's garden dried up. It was too late in the season for him to start another one. Well, he tried anyway. But it is going to be a tough winter for Hobo at the way the food prices are going up and I sure hope the damn government does something about it. Hobo must have been planning on getting married but I guess it's all off now. Poor Hobo. I guess he will have to blame Bob Fortune, the Channel 2 weather man on TV.

Then we have this nosy squirrel who lives in one of the cedars by the slough. He must have come from a better class family because he thought until a little while ago that he was better than the poorer class squirrels. He was a real bully but one day he over played his hand. He found a bird's nest and he swiped the eggs out of it. The birds knowing the delinquent's past held a hurry up conference and made their plans to way lay the bully. I watched them while they were doing it.

So Mr. Bully was starting to rob another nest and about two and a half dozen birds tackled him. It looked for a while there like they were going to tar and feather him and even worse. So Mr. Delinquent runs to my house for refuge. He ran up on to my window sill and tried to get in, all the birds in pursuit slapping Mr. Bully's ears, face and all over with their wings.

When my wife saw what was going on she did not want to get involved in harbouring a criminal and she would not open the window. Well the last time I saw Mr. Squirrel he was minding his own business. And I never see him at all on Sundays so I presume he is even going to church.

After all the high water around here from the near flooding in the spring of '72, there was clouds of mosquitoes hatched out and there was a special big one that was mean and vicious. I was batching for a spell and Mr. Mosquito tried to take advantage when I was alone. He tried to corner me but I was always a jump ahead. Finally I had to get some thing in the fridge and as I opened the fridge door Mr. Mosquito spotted the goodies inside and he flew in. To my quick thinking I shut the door quickly and I left him there for four whole hours not taking any chances. When I opened up again there was Mr. Mosquito laying on his back, shivering cold so he couldn't even raise his head. He looked so pitiful lying there so I tried to bring him around but it was too late and he died two hours later. I buried him in the garden and may he rest in peace but what I am sorry about is that I did not know at the time he was working. I found out later he was working for the Red Cross by taking people's blood and donating it. It was too late.

Couple a months ago the boys found a clutch of pheasant eggs in a little place beside the slough so they rounded up a clucking hen and she hatched them out. There were five young pheasants and they grew very quickly but Mrs. Hen had no control. They ran around so much she had no time to lecture them and I could see it worried her a lot. In a short time she was acting most strange and pretty soon we had to put her behind a screen in her own personal asylum. The poor thing didn't have a chance and she spent the rest of her life there.

Then there's a stupid sort of squirrel around here but I don't think he is a relative of Mr. Nosy Squirrel. One day by the slough I noticed these cones dropping into the water. And there he was working away up there snapping them off and dropping them down but he wasn't watching where they were landing. He was so busy gathering food he didn't even take time for a coffee break. When he figured he had enough he clumb down again and to his astonishment, when he peeked over the edge the cones were all floating in the water. He did not realize the tree was leaning out over the water. The last I saw of Mr. Stupid Squirrel he was still walking around in a circle, chattering and scratching his head.

Things aren't going so good around here. Had the TV set repaired and now the reception is worse than it was before. The neighbour's dog upsets the garbage can and also robs Little Hobo's dinner. So Hobo is gone. The birds have carried away most of the cherries and now I notice they are eyeing the black berries long before they are ripe but I suppose they have to eat too. I thought I planted some tomatoes but maybe I didn't because there are none out in the garden. The only things growing real good are the wild weeds and we sure have a good crop of them.

My wife joined the berry picking force for the first time this season but the weather man didn't. It wasn't only windy, it also rained heavily, and the Ford has packed up again and them about 17 miles from home.

The rain must have made me sleep in and that meant a cold breakfast this morning. Got my new dentures two weeks ago and they didn't help my cold breakfast any. They can't seem to learn how to chew yet. When Hobo comes back I may have to get him to soften up my food first if these damn dentures don't smarten up soon.

My family got home at noon on account of the rain. They were all soaking wet and they ate their lunches out of their lunch cans they had taken to the field. Right after that the weather man stops the wind and rain, the sun is shining bright and they have no way of getting back to work.

This is the fifth day the car has been in the shop and I am afraid to phone the garage for fear I may get the same answer, not ready yet. I picked up the phone a number of times and laid it down again. Finally I get up enough nerve to ring up the mechanic at 4:30 this afternoon and to my surprise it has been ready since noon. So now every thing is in order only the cream of the harvest crop is almost over.

To forget my troubles I turn on the TV and run into one of those exploring type programs about drugs and hippies

and kids in general. So I turned it off again. I got to thinking and I think I pin pointed the trouble. The world is all
right. It is the people who are cruel. One of our troubles
are the jones, keeping up with the jones that is. It will be
very hard to eliminate all the jones and it will take more
years than I will know.

Yesterday a friend asked me how are you feeling Hank?
So I told him about the lady running to the doctor's house
and he was in the garage working on his car. She looked
quite sick so he checked her out then and there and saw it
was an emergency case. So he laid her on the hood and
operated right there. He removed her kidney and he
replaced it with his carburator that was on the bench for
servicing because it was the only thing around at the time.
It was only going to be a temporary patch job but he forgot,
and now she is sluggish going up hill and she's hard to start
on a cold morning. That's me these days I said.

And I get a lot of headaches lately and I used to take a lot
a aspirin but the cost went up. You ask why and the answer
is always the same. Tests. Ever since I can remember seems
like they were always making aspirin tests but the more lab
tests they make the more headaches there are seems like.
Well I got my own test lab and in five minutes I had the
solution. If you get a headache all you do is stick a common
band on your forehead or your temple. It works for me.
Maybe it will for you.

Best time for me these days is when I am sleeping. That's
when I can lead a double life. Boy my wife would be mad if
she knew about it. And the secret is to have a pretty healthy
snack before bed time. The more you eat the more you
dream. Last night I dreamed that Hobo the tom cat gave
berth to four little kittens. You take it from there.

Then every so often I get these little bits of ideas and I
write them down. Want to hear some?

You can get some height by straightening out your
bowed legs.

They call it delinquency today but when I was a kid they called you a thief.

How can I exercise to be strong when I am not strong enough to exercise?

Why is it that when I put too much antifreeze in to my car's radiator my head lights get blood shot eyes?

When I put my glasses on I can't hear a thing.

The End of My Story

Well here I am almost at the end of my story. But before I sign off I want to answer the one question I get asked most of all.

Friends come around to call and sometimes when we have had one or two nearly always they say, Hank really now, what's it been like being a half breed? Tell us about it Hank.

And always the same answer I give is that it hasn't been easy. Like I said at the beginning, not white and not Indian but we look Indian and everybody except Indians takes us for Indian. I understand that there are lots of places in the world like Hawaii and the Phillipine Islands and New Zealand and places like that where a man and a woman meet up from two different breeds and they get married and have their children and nobody calls those children half breeds.

But it is different in North America and I suppose it all started when the white explorers and trappers started coming west and needing companions took up with the Indian maidens they met. Then some writers started writing about all this and putting a bad slant on the whole situation and then it became something wrong and from then on new people coming along just accepted it was wrong and didn't really think about it after that.

Then every thing got worse when the whites took all the Indian country for themselves and having to put the Indians somewhere put them on reservations. But the mistake was that only full blooded Indians could live on them and that left all kinds of half breeds to wander. And not being able to get work and no agency to look after them they became boozers and rummys and no goods and so the half breed name got even worse in the mind of the people and the different governments.

It is very bad even today. I saw on TV a couple a years ago about this lovely Eskimo maiden who married a white scientist up north and the government of Indian Affairs made her give up her rights as a Eskimo. Instead why didn't the government make the white man give up his rights? Like the Indian, the Eskimo was here first by a long time and he can trace his ancestors back a hell of a long way farther than any white man. Or instead why does the damn government interfere at all? Why shouldn't there be just people now? No Indians. No Eskimos. No whites. Just people. Maybe some day it will be like that but I know I won't be around then. Too bad because then there won't be any half breeds either and that will be a damn good thing.

Because of all the wars since 1945 look at what's happened. German people marrying American people. Canadian people marrying Jap people. Black American guys marrying Korean maidens and girls from Viet Nam and I guess their children could be named not half breeds but triple breeds. Well I don't think all this is hurting the world. I think it is mixing up everybody the way the Good Lord intended they should be because it is only a small world and it is the only world we got.

Way back in the bush amongst the big trees doing a man's work, I wasn't a half breed, I was just good old Hank working with good old Tom and good old Dick and good old Harry and we were all buddies and we watched over one another in case of a accident and we worried about one another and when one had a hangover or had wife trouble or something we covered up for him until he felt better. And I think that is the way it should be all the time for everybody.

Well when I talk like this to my friends they say come on Hank, tell us about the bootlegging instead. And what they mean is they know about the best example I can tell about being a half breed was when the liquor situation was real bad because of the Indian Act. It was all changed by a Judge Morrow[1] in the middle of the 1960's but before that for a long time it was a time when being a half breed had a good point.

But it sure was a mix up. Outside of my work I could not join the white society, socially, and if I went to a Indian party and there was liquor involved I was taking a chance of being jailed regardless of whether I had supplied them with liquor or not. If I had a Indian in the car and also a sealed bottle of whiskey or a sealed case of beer and a cop stops me on a routine check I would be charged with kniving which has several meanings like the intention of giving him a drink sooner or later.

I have been stopped by the police often when leaving a beer parlour with a couple a cases of beer under my arm, not at the door, but in my car, in case I may have a Indian with me. And taking any liquor in to a reservation was a serious offence. Us breeds used to have these documents which we got from the Indian agency saying we were non Indian and which we had to produce at liquor stores or beer parlours where we were not known.

And if you didn't buy a bottle for your Indian friends now and then pretty soon you would have no friends at all.

I remember a Saturday night when the beer parlour closed up and a couple a guys who were friends had no way to get back to the reservation that was seven miles away. I had met them when I came out standing around outside. So I gave them a ride and they had some beer with them they had picked up some wheres. Sure enough the Mounties were up the road a ways and the result was I was fined $300.

Another time I just got home maybe a half hour and I had a visit from a couple of Indian friends. We were having a quiet little drink when the Mountie walks in and I was fined another $300 for supplying. Well I said to myself, if I can't have a social drink with a Indian friend I may as well start bootlegging and get some of my money back.

Things went along pretty good and I was making a nice little piece of change when I got caught and there was another $300 to pay. So there was more money to get back.

So I took another chance. At this time I was living in Vancouver for my therapy treatments and when I would drive home to the valley on weekends I would buy up some liquor to take with me to sell. Trouble was that loggers never have any money on them so I used to let them have it on the cuff and on pay days they would always pay their bills faithful. Eventually their wives started questioning them about where the rest of their pay envelope was and one of them told the story. She told the others and they all joined forces and squealed on me. That time I was really caught proper.

Next time I did it the Mounties knew the minute I left Vancouver and three police cars ambushed me at a narrow place in the highway up the valley. As luck would have it I had a juvenile in the car who had had some drinks. And on top of that, my wife was driving so she was actually doing the transporting.

I could have been charged with all three counts, but I pleaded guilty on only one of them and got fined $300 and was let off the other two.

I can't very well blame anybody in particular. It was the system we lived under then.

So that is how it used to be being a half breed and how I think about it now. And I sure hope it will be different for these two boys of ours, Benny and Dean.

And so I guess that's all my story up to now or as much as I can remember of it and if I wanted to tell you the truth, as much as I want my wife to know about me. A man has to have some secrets.

I am glad I was born. I am glad of all I learned and the way I worked and what I worked at and I am glad to see the sun come up still and the night time to bring the night sounds. I am glad I had enough schooling to be able to write these words on paper. I feel better now because it all isn't a weight on me any more.

If I have any advice for people it is to do the best with what you got and the Lord will look after the details. I did and it looks like He did His part. And another advice is for the old timers. I would tell them to write it all down before they forget. Besides, it makes the days pass easier.

I guess I got only one more story for you.

Charlie and Joe were two Indian braves who got lost while hunting. Charlie says well Joe, what are we gonna do now? Joe thinks for a minute. Let's do white man style, fire three shots in the air. Maybe there's some body close who can help us.

So Charlie fires three shots and they listen and wait and no help arrives. Charlie says, Joe, what'll we do next? Joe says fire three more shots. So Charlie fires three more shots.

Well, time was running out. It was getting dusky. Now what says Charlie. Joe said fire three more shots. I can't says Charlie, I haven't any more arrows left.

And there you have it.

Y'rs truly

[Hank Pennier]

P.S. write me a letter some time.

Glossary of Logging Terms

bent (45)   A cluster of pilings used to support a bridge or trestle.

bill of lading (23)   A transport document that confirms receipt of goods. Goods are released only after presentation and handing over of a correctly endorsed original bill of lading.

bucker and faller (55)   A bucker cuts a felled tree into lengths; a faller fells trees. Typically, a faller is also a bucker, but the same does not necessarily apply in reverse. Both were dangerous jobs, especially in the era before chainsaws, and to this day fallers have the highest prestige jobs in the logging industry, although for second growth trees much of the falling is now done by robotic machines.

bull car (37)   The first (closest to the engine) in a line of flat cars. The Bull Car is equipped with a manual brake to stop the line of flat cars.

bull cook (55)   Typically an older or permanently injured logging camp worker responsible for cleaning bunkhouses, building fires, doing dishes, and other odd jobs.

bull of the woods (36)   A term of respect bestowed by loggers on a tougher than usual camp foreman, boss, or superintendent.

choker (33)   A cable sling for encircling the end of a log

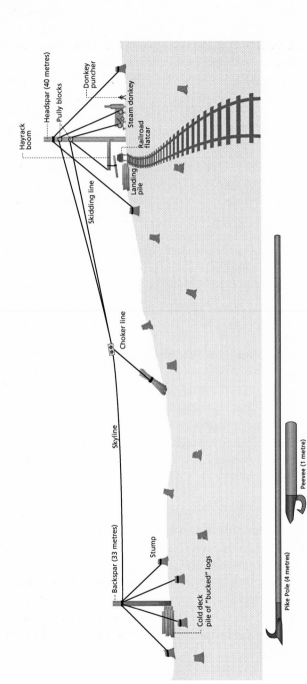

Spar tree steam logging operation. Drawn by Jan Perrier, based largely upon diagrams found in Richard Mackie, *Island Timber* (Victoria: Sono Nis Press, 2000), 190, 224.

so it can be yarded away. The choker cable has a knob on the end that wraps around the log and is cinched tight with the kow going through the bell. A chokerman was responsible for setting the choker cable.

donkey engineer (46)   The steam engineer responsible for overseeing operation of a steam donkey. Also known as a yarder engineer or a donkey puncher.

faller (23)   Fells trees. Saws or chops an undercut on one side of a tree to determine the direction of the fall (to minimize damage to the timber) and then backcuts the opposite side to actually fell (drop) the tree.

freshet (6)   Highwater time, when rain or snow melt causes the river to swell and spill over its banks and flood.

gypo logging camp (55)   A small private logging company, typically with a single tower and loader, operating on a shoestring budget while seeking short-term profits. Generally considered a business not worth investing in. Today the term gypo is often disparagingly applied to contract non-union loggers and truck drivers. 'Gypo' or 'gyppo' (pronounced 'jippo') is presumably a derogatory derivation of 'gypsy.'

head loader (56)   Responsible for overseeing the loading logs from the landing to the railroad flatcars. His primary task was to ensure the logs were balanced. The 'second loader' set the 90-lb. tongs (or the ¾-inch cable if the tongs were too small for the log).

high rigger (66)   The senior rigger, responsible for climbing, topping, limbing, and rigging the spar tree. He rigged the guidelines for the spar tree, setting the 800-lb. bull block for the main line, and the 200-lb. haul-back block for the return line.

high rigging (25)   Cables and blocks associated with spar tree logging where logs were hauled high into the air to enable them to be yarded freely back to the landing.

hogger (43)   Steam locomotive engineer. Also known as a hoghead.

hook tender (66)   Foreman of a yarding crew, responsible for supervising movement of logs from forest to landing.

loading engineer (50)   Worker responsible for overseeing the 'loading' or 'landing' crew of a skidder operation; separate from the yarder.

loci engineer (43)   A loci was a slang term for steam locomotive. The loci engineer operated the lead machine in a yarding operation.

Loggers' Employment Agency (LEA) (55)   Essentially a hiring hall formed by coastal logging companies under the auspices of the BC Loggers' Association in response to the strikes organized by the British Columbia Loggers' Union (later known as the Lumber Workers' Industrial Union) throughout the spring and summer of 1919. The Loggers' Employment Agency kept an active list of union organizers and all men who had participated in the 1919 strikes. According to one account, by 1922 the LEA was maintaining a blacklist of roughly 1,500 names. The LEA controlled employment in the coastal logging industry well into the 1940s. (See Gordon Hak, 'British Columbia Loggers and the Lumber Workers' Industrial Union, 1919–1922,' *Labour/Le Travail* 23 [Spring 1989]: 67–90.)

monkey action gear (60)   Valve gear linkage on a steam locomotive that requires 'gear dope' for lubrication.

monkey wrench (61)   General purpose mechanic. The term is derived from the name of the inventor of the 'monkey wrench' tool, Charles Moncky. The monkey wrench is adjustable and can therefore be used on a variety of nuts. Invented in the mid-nineteenth century, the monkey wrench is also now more commonly known as the crescent wrench.

peevee hook (25)   Also spelled 'peavey.' A six-foot long-handled tool with sharp point and moveable cant hook that creates leverage in order to move or role logs on hillsides or in the water of a booming ground.

pike pole (73)   Long pole tipped with a spike and small hook used by boom men to sort and direct logs in a river or holding pond.

powder monkey (14)   Worker who sets explosive charges.

rolling stock (47)   Railroad cars and engines belonging to a steam logging company.

salt chuck (60)   'Chuck' is Chinook jargon for 'water.' The salt chuck is the ocean, a term still in use among residents of small towns along the British Columbia coast.

scow (47)   Flat-bottomed barge similar in design to a punt.

Shay loci (60)   Noisy steam locomotive designed specifically for logging by former logger Ephriam Shay (1839–1916). Two features made the Shay distinctive: a gear drive in place of a side rod drive, and an unusual rapid-fire vertical cylinder arrangement. Together these features allowed the Shay to negotiate heavy grades and sharp curves that would have stymied regular side rod locomotives. The Shay loci went into commercial production in 1880 and remained a mainstay of the logging industry through to the 1940s.

siding (51)   Short line of railroad track running parallel to the main line, where cars and engines can pull over out of the way of vehicles passing in the other direction.

skidder (37)   Machine with a spool drum or winch used to move logs or trees to the landing in place of a yarder.

skidder lines (45)   By the 1940s skidders had begun to replace donkeys in the coastal logging industry. The first skidders were mounted on flatcars. They had separate engines for yarding and loading. Skidder lines were the highlead cables running from the skidder to the yarding equipment.

spar tree (55)   Tall limbed tree, rigged for highlead, skyline, or slackline 'cable-haul' yarding.

speeder (57)   Small self-powered four-wheeled vehicle that runs on a railroad track. Used principally to carry workers to and from a work site, and by maintenance workers conducting repairs. The speeder took the place of the handcar, and has in turn been succeeded by modified pickup trucks adapted with both rubber tires and steel railroad wheels that are lowered by hydraulic pump.

stakey (33)   Logger who had made a 'stake,' one who had the urge to quit the logging camp and go to town to spend his money, usually 'binge spending' with little consideration for the consequences. The term also seems to have applied to the 'gandy dancer' who repaired the railroad tracks.

standing stick (73)   Log reaching from the shore to the booming grounds, used as a sort of sidewalk by workers on the booming grounds.

steam certificate (46)   Professional journeyman's certificate issued to steam engineers.

steam cold deckers (37)   Cold decker was the name used to describe a mobile donkey engine mounted on a sled. It was used to yard logs and stack them within reach of the skidder.

steam donkey engine (25)   Stationary steam-powered drum (or spool) engine with an upright boiler used for yarding logs. Also called a steam pot. Typically burned seven chords of wood per day.

steam pot (25)   Another name for a steam donkey engine.

steam railroad show (42)   Steam railroad logging operation. In coastal BC, steam logging was the most common form of forest resource extraction from the late 1800s to the end of the Second World War.

straw line (42)   Light cordage rope (later replaced with ¼-inch cable) used to pull the main line cables into place.

whistle punk (56)   Entry level position in the early to mid-twentieth-century logging industry. A whistle punk was the member of the rigging crew who signalled the donkey puncher when to start and stop the engine during yarding with a jerk wire hooked to a steam whistle.

yarder engineer (36) Operator of a donkey. Also known as a donkey engineer or a donkey puncher.

yarding (36) The process of moving logs from where they are felled to the landing where they were loaded onto railcars (and later trucks).

Appendix 1
Hank's Grandfather,
George John Perrier

George Perrier was born in Montreal and served as a sailor with the Hudson's Bay Company. He arrived in BC in the late 1850s and quickly left the company's employ to seek his fortunes in California. When rumours reached San Francisco that there was gold to be had on the gravel bars of the Fraser River, Perrier was among the first to head north. There, on the shores of the Fraser, Perrier founded a lucrative corporation that diverted water from a creek through a ditch to supply placer mines at Hill's Bar. His connections with the Honourable Company served him well when in the spring of 1858 the former HBC chief-factor-turned-colonial-governor, James Douglas, arrived at the mouth of the Fraser Canyon to confront a group of American miners who, either challenging or ignoring the Queen's authority, had established a form of local republican-style self-government at Hill's Bar. After disbanding the American council, Douglas reportedly approached George Perrier and asked him if he 'understood law.' Responding affirmatively, the former HBC sailor explained that he had in fact read *Commentaries on the Law of England* by the noted British jurist Sir William Blackstone. 'Tut-tut,' the Governor supposedly replied. 'It's not Blackstone you want here but just common sense.' And with that as his interview, Perrier was summarily appointed justice of the peace with the authority to arrest British subjects, local Aboriginals, and foreign nationals alike.[1]

From his position as magistrate of Hill's Bar, Hank's grandfather George Perrier played a brief but prominent role in British Columbia's early colonial history and the history of Native–newcomer relations. After appointing Perrier, Douglas had assured the local Aboriginal population that British law would protect their rights no less than those of the white man, and further, he instructed them to apply to Perrier for redress whenever wronged by white men. In the summer of 1858 dealings between the predominantly American mining population and the local indigenous population had become seriously strained and Douglas's promises, along with Perrier's abilities, would be put to the test. In just four short months from April to July, more than 30,000 miners had arrived in the Fraser Canyon where they quickly earned indigenous ire for their dismissive attitude toward Aboriginal land rights and their often violent and exploitative behaviour toward Native women. By August the isolated conflicts had escalated into open warfare. Organized militias of miners razed ancient settlements and desecrated burials, while Aboriginal warriors routed placer mine camps. Lives were lost on both sides, and the situation appeared to be spiralling out of control until the Stó:lō and Nlakapamux leaders Liquitim and Spintlem began to conduct independent peace talks with a level-headed and influential American miner named Snyder. The process was not an easy one, however. Two weeks earlier, a delegation of Aboriginal leaders who arrived in Yale to begin negotiating a cessation of violence were accosted by a rowdy mob. Were it not for the bold and decisive actions of Magistrate Perrier, a Native delegate known as Suseechus would have been lynched.

Despite his actions on behalf of the Aboriginal treaty delegates and his former HBC affiliation, Perrier maintained and nurtured close associations with the overwhelmingly American population at Hill's Bar. This relationship inevitably led him into conflict with his counterpart, the magistrate across the river at Yale. The rivalry came to a head following an incident on Christmas day, 1858: a drunken resident of Hill's Bar severely pistol-whipped an African-American barber at Yale. When the Yale magistrate dispatched one of his constables across the river to arrest the alleged perpetrator, Perrier chose to pass the warrant to his own officers and conduct the trial himself at Hill's Bar. Under advice from the accused assailant's good friend and notorious Californian vigilance leader Ned McGowan (whose influence over the Hill's Bar community was comparable to Al Capone's over 1920s Chicago), Perrier determined that he could not complete the trial until he had interviewed the victim of the crime. He summarily issued his own warrant for the beaten barber, who was then being held in protective custody in the Yale jail. The Yale magistrate, however, refused to recognize Perrier's jurisdiction on his side of the river and instead incarcerated the Hill's Bar police officer on charges of contempt of court. When Perrier attempted to have both prisoners transferred to his Hill's Bar court, the Yale official refused. On McGowan's advice, Perrier then deputized McGowan and nine others and sent them to Yale to retrieve both prisoners, and to arrest the Yale justice of the peace on yet another charge of contempt of court. Perrier's forces were successful, and justice was dispensed in the Hill's Bar courtroom: the perpetrator of the assault on the barber was fined seventy-five dollars, the arresting constable acquitted, and the Yale magistrate found guilty of contempt and fined fifty dollars. After the trial, Perrier used the fifty dollars to buy 'drinks all around' for the Hill's Bar residents as they celebrated New Year's. Indignant letters from the Yale magistrate following the trial convinced Douglas to dispatch a contingent of Royal Engineers to Yale to assess the situation. Hearing of developments, Perrier travelled to intercept the advancing soldiers and successfully ingratiated himself with the colony's new military commander, Col. R.C. Moody, and Chief Justice Mathew Bailey Begbie, convincing them that he had acted only under 'great provocation.' Such was not sufficient, however, to excuse his behaviour, and Perrier was dismissed for what one early historian characterized as having 'strain[ed] the point of legal dignity.'[2]

Disgraced but not discouraged, Perrier then returned to his lucrative ditch company before re-ingratiating himself with colonial authorities and securing the contract to build the trail between Hill's Bar and Fort Hope. His reputation largely restored, Perrier soon thereafter resumed his position near the centre of BC's colonial social roster. In 1861 he became a celebrated thespian playing a leading role in the colony's first amateur theatrical performance, a comic musical titled 'Sent to the Tower.' In 1862 he returned to the stage in the locally written and produced 'On Derby Day, or Miss Smith.' Later that year Perrier followed the gold trail north to the Caribou where he caught the attention of the colonial secretary after tracking down two notorious horse thieves and then returning the purloined steed to its rightful owner. Perrier's luck continued to run hot and cold, however, for a few months later his dry goods store was reportedly burglarized and then set ablaze while Perrier was out courting a young woman. Discouraged, Hank's grandfather then returned to Yale where he built and then operated the Colonial Hotel and Restaurant. A few years later he was homesteading on the fertile banks of the Harrison River, and it was there, presumably, that he met and married Hank's grandmother, Suzanne Chiltlat. When and where Perrier met his end is unknown. Hank claims he was shot by a business partner while on a trip to Quebec. Those living descendants of George Perrier we have spoken with have no knowledge of such an affair, nor has corroborating evidence been found in archival sources. What is clear, however, is that the Hank Pennier inherited some of his colourful grandfather's joie de vivre.[3]

Appendix 2
A Conversation with Hank in
His Kitchen, 16 October 1972[1]

In 1972 the Stó:lō community of Skowkale in Chilliwack British Columbia launched the Skulkayn Heritage Project. Over a two-year period, young indigenous researchers interviewed and recorded conversations with numerous Stó:lō elders throughout the Fraser Valley on a host of topics. Some elders chose to discuss political issues. Others told ancient stories of community genesis and subsequent miraculous transformations. Still others discussed their personal and family histories. Sometimes they just talked.

Most of the conversations were conducted in English, but a significant number were in the Halq'eméylem language. Over the years the tapes have proven an invaluable source of genealogical, linguistic, cultural, and historical information for Stó:lō families and outside scholars alike.

Some of the interviews were conducted one-on-one. More typically there were two or more researchers asking an elder questions. Moreover, because the interviews were conducted informally, usually in an elder's home, it was not uncommon for there to be other voices on the tape – those of the elder's family members or guests who dropped by for a visit part way through the interview. Sometimes these other voices participate in the conversations, either by assisting the elders in answering questions, or; more frequently, by asking additional questions of their own. More than thirty years after the fact, it is not always possible for contemporary listeners to identify all the voices. In the transcribed interview presented below, a man and a woman ask Hank most of the questions, but there are other people in the kitchen as well, and they too sometimes become involved. For ease of reading, we have identified only Hank's voice by name; the other voices we have conflated simply as 'other.' With the exception of certain unintelligible words and a few minutes of conversation between two of the other people in the room that did not involve Hank directly, the transcript is complete. Such edits and omissions are represented with an ellipse within brackets [...]. To assist readers we have added subheadings and provided cross-referencing page numbers indicating where versions of the stories can also be found within Hank's written text.

Publishing the Book

HANK: I got a letter from Susie, but I haven't got an answer from my last letter. She was all excited about my book.

OTHER: How long did it take you to write that book?

HANK: Well, that's hard to say, ahhh...

OTHER: When did you start?

HANK: Oh, about four years ago I guess. But this guy I was working with, he went to Edinborough for about two years, so there was a gap there. Then when I started reading my own stories, God it made me laugh. Geez. After two years I'd forgot [what I wrote], you know.

OTHER: So you just now started selling that book.

HANK: Yes, just in September [1972].

OTHER: So that's about two months now.

HANK: Yeah.

OTHER: So you can't get no money yet?

HANK: Oh about next year, about September. Well, there's more to it than the printing.

OTHER: How much does it cost that guy? About $10,000 to get it published?

HANK: Close to $10,000 to get it published.

OTHER: So he's got to get his money back first before they pay you.[2]

HANK: Yeah, it's got to be registered in Ottawa. You cannot just write a book and start selling it. Well I get 10% now – for the first 5,000. After that I'll get 12[%], and then 15[%]. The more they sell the better.

OTHER: Billy Sepass has a book out. I ordered it. *Sepass Poems.*[3]

HANK: Well that's nice. [...]

Matches and Ghosts

HANK: Well there's one good story that I told Pat Charlie – from Katz,[4] you know?

OTHER: My uncle.

HANK: Yeah. Well they were pretty strict. You know, the priest gathered all the Indians near the church. They had watchmen and chiefs watching over everything.[5] Well, Pat Charlie,[6] he went up a ladder to the second floor. He put this ladder up there. Someone spotted the ladder and told the chief. They all surrounded this building. Well, they used to have these Chinese matches, I don't know if you've ever seen them. Sulphur matches. You know, they were about the size of your thumb, and they were like toothpicks. Well, he had one of those in his pocket. He was going to get caught, and had to get out somehow. Well, he spit on his hand and he rubbed the sulphur matches around on his hand and he put some on his face. And there was a guy down at the foot of the steps, standing there. He was waiting for him come down. He was going to nail him. Well, he looked up and he thought he saw a ghost. The phosphorous made his face glow. He beat it. Well, they all beat it! [*Laughter*]

Making Cider (see page 17)

HANK: You know Webster, I guess you know him.
OTHER: Yeah. Um hm.
HANK: One time, you know, the fall of the year, he had an orchard there. I'm gonna make cider, he says to himself. Had a great big barrel, picked these apples real careful, filled that barrel up, covering it. On and on, thought the cider would be ready by Christmas, you know. 'It's time to tap that barrel.' He went there with dipper and glasses, they were gonna drink right there, you know, had this big barrel. Webster[7] opened this thing, apples are still whole. [*Laughter*]

Sign of the Cross

HANK: I was first teaching a couple of our grandchildren how to pray, you know?
OTHER: Who was teaching them?
HANK: This old lady from Katz Landing. This was many years ago. 'Go pray for a little while.' Then the little one started to cry. I asked her, 'What's going on?' She must have been praying the sign of the cross. The little one said, 'Oh, he hit me right in the Holy Ghost!' [*Laughter*]

No Communion, and Salt in the Priest's Coffee
(see page 10)

HANK: Yeah, I got in my book there too, the time I was serving mass at Seabird [Island].[8] That's the year Liv Charles, my friend, was getting married – 1919. I was serving mass and the bishop was there. And I was the first one supposed to receive communion; you know, [I was the] altar boy. And I genuflect in the middle there. Father Chirouse,[9] he was the one doing the communion. Tongue out, eyes closed, then I get tired. Bugger went by me. Looking back [I could see] he was giving them other Indians communion. [*Laughter*] I was tired, waiting.

OTHER: All by yourself?

HANK: Yeah. Father Chirouse, he was quite a guy.

OTHER: He was quite a guy, Father Chirouse.

HANK: I give him salt one time with his tea.

OTHER: For his tea? [*Laughter*]

HANK: Yeah. Well, I got the story about that; but, ahh, got it worded different. This happened up at Union Bar, we had a dinner outside. You know it's little different in my book, you know, you gotta change.

OTHER: Yeah.

HANK: That was a nice day and quite a gathering up at my mother's place. Had the tables set outside. Father Chirouse, he was at the head and I was next, and my brother Laurence was on the other corner. And the saltshaker, I mean the salt was in one of them big fucking saltshakers, so I grabbed this salt, put it closer. He thought it was sugar, I guess. It was in a thing like those big ashtrays, you know? I watched as he made this strange face [*laughter*], and then he tried a little and it didn't taste right, and put another scoop, more in. Oh, what he must have [thought]. 'Whaaaaaa!' [*Laughter*] I guess he would of swore but he couldn't, he was a priest. [*Laughter*] He never let me sit near him after that. [*Laughter*]

Skulls (see pages 15–16)

HANK: We use to play with them skulls, when they was building the CNR.[10] Along the track behind Union Bar, there. I guess they were old warriors, you know. Those guys building the track just left the skulls lying there. Well, we found them and I used to use them for footballs [*nervous laughter*]. My stepfather caught us, and geez he was mad. He gathered them and went and buried them up at the cemetery.

[...]

OTHER: Probably they were Xwithwilh skulls.

HANK: Yes, they were different. Xwithwilh skulls.

OTHER: Whereabouts were those skulls? Whereabouts were the skulls?

HANK: You now where the track is? Well, between the graveyard and the where Frisco lives. You know where they were digging those big holes there for the track? Between Frisco Gutierrez' crossing and where the cemetery is now. By the mountains, like.

OTHER: In the 1948 flood the water came right up over the floor in your mother's house where we were living. We had to move in Gutierrez' chicken house for the whole summer [...]

HANK: There's a person buried right straight out from the main graveyard there. He was supposed to have small-pox, I think. They buried him outside. Toward the railroad tracks. You know where the graveyard is – straight out. One time I was with my sister, and I were walking, going up to see my mother, and we heard somebody crying. We wondered where the grave was. [We heard it] over by the grave-yard. Sounded like maybe my mother, you know. And we got to the house and she wasn't in there. And it was day-time. 'What the hell?' Whether it came from that grave or not, it came from that area.

Notes

Introduction to 2006 Edition

1 Suzanne was not the first Aboriginal woman Perrier had pursued. During the gold rush he had unsuccessfully courted the mixed-blood daughter of Fort Yale's chief trader, Ovid Allard.

2 The new name's French spelling is likely a reflection of the French Oblate missionaries' efforts to render into their baptismal and marriage records the Stó:lõ pronunciation of 'Perrier.' Interestingly, the next generation of literate English-speaking Stó:lõ transformed the name once again – likely on the basis of the pronunciation of English vowels. Thus, Perrier becomes Pennier, and Pennier becomes pronounced 'Pen-i-yer,' or as Hank renders it, 'Pennee-err.'

3 Franz Boas renders the name 'Suwilä'si$\ddot{a}$' in 'Indian Tribes of the Lower Fraser River,' 454).

4 Hank's stepbrother Alan Gutierrez, of the Chawathil reserve just down river from Hope, now carries the name Swallsea. Alan's wife, Matilda (one of two remaining fluent Halq'eméylem speakers), explains that the name refers to the 'rising and turning' of the little water people, who originally owned the Sxwó:yxwey mask when they were fished from the waters of the 'lake-within-the-Fraser-river' to reveal the mask to the Stó:lõ people for the first time. Alan explains that the hereditary name Swallsea was transferred to him by his grandfather Billy while the latter lay on his deathbed.

5 We are grateful to Hank's son 'Jumbo,' his niece Patricia, and genealogist Alice Marwood for their assistance in sorting out Hank's ancestry and family tree.

6 See, for example, *Stalo Nation News*, 'Biography of Hank Pennier.'

7 Knight, *Indians at Work*.

8 See, for example, Krech, *The Ecological Indian*; Nash, *Wilderness and the American Mind*; Oelschlaeger, *The Idea of Wilderness*.

9 See, for example, the discussion and illustration of such a contest between a Stó:lō man and a grizzly in Carlson with McHalsie, *'I Am Stó:lō!'* 90.

10 Holden, 'Making All the Crooked Ways Straight,' 272. For a more theoretical discussion of similar narrative techniques among African-American writers, see Gates, *The Signifying Monkey*.

11 Appendix 2, this volume, 103.

12 See Carlson, 'Reflections on Indigenous History and Memory.'

13 King, *The Truth about Stories*, 166, 154.

14 Holden, 'Making All the Crooked Ways Straight,' 272.

15 Hilbert, 'Poking Fun in Looshootseed,' 198.

16 Deloria, *Custer Died for Your Sins*, 169.

17 Hawthorn, ed., *A Survey of the Contemporary Indians*, 2:8.

18 For more contemporary, but similarly sympathetic (or softly critical), accounts of either St Mary's Catholic Residential School or Coqualeetza Methodist Residential School, see Glavin, *Amongst God's Own*; McIvor, *Coqualeetza*; and Raibmon, '"A New Understanding of Things Indian."' For more extended and critical appraisals of British Columbia and Canadian residential schools in general, consult Haig-Brown, *Resistance and Renewal*, and Miller, *Shingwauk's Vision*.

19 Lawrence, review of *Chiefly Indian*, 125.

20 See, for example, Dion's posthumous *My Tribe the Crees*, along with less well-known works like Wapiti's *Ashes of the Fire*.

Foreword to 1972 Edition

1 The linguistic study of sounds and pronunciation.

2 The language of the Coast Salish people living along the lower Fraser River watershed of southwestern British Columbia and the adjacent shores of southeastern Vancouver Island. The Halkomelem language is divided into three major dialect groups: Halq'eméylem, Hun'qumyi'num, and Hul'q'umín'um (popularly referred to as Upriver, Downriver, and Island, respectively).

3 Nicomen is an English corruption of Leq'á:mél (the tide comes in), the name associated with the large island on the Fraser River adjacent to Mission City, BC, where Hank Pennier and his wife Margaret were living when Roberts first visited him. This site marks the approximate up-river extent of tidal fluctuations in water level on the Fraser River.

4 Will Rogers was a popular cowboy comedian who, like Hank Pennier, incorporated his mixed Aboriginal-European ancestry into his humour. Rogers appeared in vaudeville and radio programs throughout the 1920s and early 1930s. Rogers's preferred comedic medium was the anecdote, just as it was for Pennier, in which he provided insightful and ironic commentaries on contemporary American society and politics. Among his most memorable lines are 'My ancestors didn't come over on the *Mayflower*, but they met the boat,' and 'Everybody is ignorant. Only on different subjects.' Harry Golden had a similar style but one that was more urban in content.

Prologue to 1972 Edition

1 Typically used to describe a member of the Chehalis tribe/band, but could also apply to residents of neighboring Scowlitz. The Chehalis and Scowlitz are Stó:lō Coast Salish people whose traditional homelands are centred in their villages on the shores of the Harrison River.

Part 1

1 Sts'aí:les ('lying on chest' like a heart). A Stó:lō community located on the Harrison River.

2 A non-Native settlement just east of Mission City in the Fraser Valley. The name Hatzic is an English corruption of the Halkomelem term Xa:t'suq – a reference to the 'sacred bulrushes' that grew in the shallow waters there. When mispronounced as Hatzic, the word sounds like the Halq'eméylem term 'measuring the penis.'

3 The HBC's *Beaver* was the first steamship to ply the waters off the west coast of what is now Canada and the United States. This sidewheeler made its appearance in 1835 and remained in active service until it ran aground at the entrance to Vancouver Harbour in 1888. A sternwheel steamer of the same name was a regular passenger/supply ship between Vancouver and Yale in the late nineteenth century.

4 Hops, which adds flavour to beer, became a major cash crop in the Fraser Valley in the late nineteenth century. The aromatic hop blossom dries and becomes a ripe cone in September, and Aboriginal people provided the majority of the labour needed for seasonal harvest until automation began to replace human pickers in the 1950s. The last Fraser Valley hop yard closed in 1996. See also Robert L.A. Hancock, 'The Hop Yards: Work Place and Social Place,' 70–1.

5 The Stó:lō community of Iwówes located on the shores of the Fraser River between Hope and Yale at the mouth of the Coquihalla River. Its current English name is derived from the name American gold miners assigned to their temporary mining campsite adjacent to the gravel bar at that location during the rush of 1858.

6 The rising floodwaters of the lower Fraser River associated with the late-spring, early-summer melting of snow in the inland headwaters of the Fraser River.

7 The Yokoughltegh or 'Lekwiltok' people are Kwakwaka'wakw speakers from the Cape Mudge area of southern Johnstone

and northern Georgia Straits near the northeast end of
Vancouver Island. Historically there was much animosity
between the Lekwiltok and the Salish of Georgia Strait and
the lower Fraser River. This feeling was greatly accented when
the Lekwiltok acquired guns from American maritime traders
ca. 1800.

8 Iwówes, known in English as Union Bar. (See note 5.)

9 Steam-powered vessels propelled by large circular paddles
located on the rear (stern) of the ship. In the nineteenth century, sternwheelers could navigate up the Fraser River as far
as the falls just beyond the town of Yale (the entrance to the
Fraser Canyon). It was at Yale that the Cariboo Road leading
to the BC plateau interior began.

10 This particular whirlpool is renowned in Stó:lō history. It is
called Hemq'eleq, which translates roughly as 'being
devoured by the water.' Like the famous geyser Old Faithful
in Yellowstone Park, Hemq'eleq disappears and then reap-
pears roughly every ninety seconds. At its peak, the
Hemq'eleq whirlpool is over twenty metres in diameter with a
centre 'hole' that drops roughly two metres below the level of
the surrounding water. Hemq'eleq literally devours anything
that is unfortunate enough to be caught in its vortex. In the
past, Stó:lō people considered Hemq'eleq somewhat of a
guardian. Locals knew to beware, but unsuspecting coastal
raiders often found themselves and their giant canoes
devoured by Hemq'eleq's powerful currents and dragged to
the bottom of the Fraser River.

11 The colloquial term used by Stó:lō people to refer to St
Mary's residential school, the federally funded Roman Catholic institution located in Mission, BC. St Mary's was opened in
1863 by the Oblates of Mary Immaculate.

12 A popular designation for the inhabitants of the four
Stl'atl'imx (Lillooet Salish) settlements along the lower Lillooet River near the old steamboat port at the head of Harrison lake (named after BC colonial governor James Douglas).
Collectively, these Stl'atlimx communities are often referred

to as the In-shuk-ch. Stó:lō oral traditions suggest that this area was occupied by Halq'eméylem speakers prior to the smallpox epidemic of the late eighteenth century.

13 The non-Native community located near the junction of the Fraser and Harrison rivers just across Harrison Bay from the Scowlitz Indian Reserve. A sawmill operated here in the past.

14 A large flat-bottomed barge-like ferry directed by guidelines.

15 Here Hank is referring to the difference between the 'flattened' skulls and the unmodified 'round' skulls that were popular among many Northwest Coast Aboriginal communities at times prior to the twentieth century. The flattened (or 'pointed') effect was created by binding infants' heads to their cradleboard for the first few weeks after their birth. At certain times in history the resulting permanent high sloping forehead designated membership in the upper class of coastal society. At European contact, the upriver Stó:lō elite were no longer flattening skulls, while people living downriver and along the coast were. Thus what Hank describes as a geographic difference was in fact largely a temporal variation in style.

16 Here Hank is applying the popular name of the 1957 flu epidemic to his discussion of the 1918 epidemic. The Asian Flu of 1957 killed between one and four million people in Europe and North America. Though the 1957 epidemic was terrible, the Spanish Flu epidemic of 1918 (which Hank discusses) was far worse. It is estimated that the Spanish Flu killed twenty million people worldwide – more than died in the trenches of the First World War.

17 The sale of alcohol to Aboriginal people was one of the earliest concerns of the Vancouver Island and British Columbia colonial legislatures in the 1850s and 1860s respectively. The prohibition continued after confederation with Canada and was not altered until 1951, when amendments to the Indian Act allowed Aboriginal people to consume alcohol in accordance with provincial regulations – but not in public. It was

not until 1970 that Aboriginal people acquired full and equal rights with non-Natives concerning alcohol. The earliest introduction of alcohol to British Columbia Aboriginal people occurred during the maritime fur trade of the late eighteenth century. Once the land-based fur trade supplanted the maritime trade (ca.1830s), the sale of alcohol to Aboriginal people was severely curtailed – the Hudson's Bay Company officially opposed the sale of intoxicating liquors to Aboriginal people. It was during the early years of the colony of Vancouver Island, and then especially during the 1858 Fraser River gold rush, that alcohol became readily available to coastal Aboriginal people – often with disastrous effects. Hank and other Aboriginal people were also affected by other prohibition legislation that at times was applied more broadly to Native and newcomers alike. For a time in the 1920s the BC provincial government prohibited the sale of alcohol to anyone except for medical purposes.

Part 2

1 Kettle Valley Railroad engineer Andrew McCulloch engineered the complex string of 'Quintette Tunnels' running through the Coquihalla Canyon just east of Hope, BC, in 1910. The railroad was designed to provide a western link to the Kootenay silver mines of southeastern BC. McCulloch, a fan of Shakespeare, named each of the stations along the railway after characters from the Bard's plays. The areas along the Kettle Valley railroad were traditional berry-picking sites for both the Stó:lō and Nlakapamux First Nations people.
2 A 'company store' where employees could purchase goods on credit, or commission.
3 Stumping refers to the arduous task of pulling stumps up by the roots to make the land suitable for other purposes. Typically, after a tree was felled, the roots of the stump were exposed and cut, then a cable was placed around the stump and attached either to a team of horses or other draft ani-

mals, or to a mechanical levered device anchored to another stump.

4 The colloquial non-Native designation for the southern communities of the Chilliwack Tribe of Stó:lō Aboriginal people living in Sardis, BC, in the Fraser Valley.

Part 3

1 It was illegal for Aboriginal people to purchase or consume alcohol in 1931, and so some Aboriginal people made and consumed their own homemade alcoholic brews. 'Home brew' was a derogatory expression used to describe an Aboriginal alcoholic who got drunk on home-brewed beer or home-distilled alcohol. Harrison River Home Brews was the pejorative term for alcoholics from Indian reserves along the Harrison River.

2 Another slang term for alcoholics.

3 An engineer certified in the operation of the powerful air-brakes used on railroad logging equipment.

4 During the 1930s depression the Canadian government established work camps, known as 'relief camps,' for unemployed men. In exchange for hard manual labour men received three square meals, a place to sleep, and twenty cents per day.

5 Long before the arrival of Europeans, Salish women mixed clay with the wool of mountain goats and of specially bred 'woolly dogs,' to weave ornate blankets called in Halq'eméylem 'léxwtel.' After the arrival of non-Native settlers, Salish women began producing European-style sweaters with unique indigenous animal and geometric designs. By the mid-twentieth century these sweaters were finding a ready commercial market in the large urban centres of Vancouver and Victoria. The hub of what was often termed the Indian sweater industry was the Cowichan Salish community near Duncan on Vancouver Island, where dozens of women knit sweaters to supplement their family's income – hence the name 'Cowichan sweater.'

Part 4

1 An expression used to describe the process whereby the bottom (butt) of a big first-growth tree flips up in a dangerous fashion as it is felled.

2 A cogwheel is a gear with teeth (cogs) that engage the cogs of another larger or smaller wheel in order to change the speed or direction of a series of gears. A loose nut thrown into a cogwheel would damage the cogs and render the wheel useless. Thus, this colloquial expression refers to someone who not only does not belong, but is damaging to the harmonious relationship among other workers.

3 The Fraser River has twice in recent memory flooded so severely that serious loss of life and property has resulted. The first and largest flood occurred in 1894, the second in 1948. Following each of these events the system of dykes protecting Fraser Valley farms and communities was upgraded and improved. Indian reserves, as federal land, were beyond the concern of the provincial government and as such were the last of the habituated sites along the lower Fraser waterway to be protected from flooding. Some Stó:lō reserves did not receive dykes until the 1970s.

4 'Chuck' is Chinook jargon for water. The ocean continues to be referred to by people in the coastal logging and fishing industry as the 'salt chuck' or simply, 'the chuck.'

Part 5

1 Judge Morrow ruled (1967) that the Indian Act prohibition that made it an offence for an Indian to be intoxicated off a reserve was a violation of the Canadian Bill of Rights. His decision, made in Yellowknife, was upheld by the Supreme Court of Canada, which rejected the Crown's appeal in *Regina v. Drybones* (1970), and the Indian Act was amended accordingly.

Appendix 1

1 James Moore, 'The Discovery of Gold on Hill's Bar in 1858.'
Significantly, Douglas also named a number of Stó:lõ men to
the same position with authority to arrest and bring to British
justice members of their own Aboriginal community.
2 Hubert Howe Bancroft, *History of British Columbia, 1792–1887*.
See also Donald Hauka's *McGowan's War*.
3 We are grateful to Mabel (Lawrence) Nichols for sharing her
knowledge and notes about her great-grandfather George
Perrier.

Appendix 2

1 We are grateful to Hank's son 'Jumbo' for sharing his copy of
this recording of his father with us, and for allowing us to
reproduce it here for others to read.
2 Herbert I. McDonald was the editor and publisher of Hank's
book, *Chiefly Indian*.
3 Unlike Hank's personal accounts of relatively contemporary
times, *Sepass Tales* is a collection of legendary stories of
ancient genesis and transformation. William Sepass (K'hhal-
serten) was born ca. 1840 into his father's Okanagan community near Coleville, Washington. His mother was Nlakapamux
from the Fraser Canon in British Columbia. Following a mea-
sles epidemic, young William relocated to Chilliwack, BC, to
be near his mother's mother's relatives. There, on the
Skowkale Indian Reserve and under the mentorship of his
high-status uncle Khal-agh-thi-til, Sepass became one of the
most prominent and respected Stó:lõ leaders of the late nineteenth and early twentieth centuries. It was in 1911 that he
approached Eloise Street, the daughter of Methodist missionaries, and apparently asked her to translate his family's
ancient stories into English so they could be put in a book
and preserved for all time. According to Street, they worked
on the project haltingly until 1915. The stories then remained

in manuscript form until the year after Sepass's death in 1943.
At that time, Street submitted them to Ryerson's for publication. Anthropologist Marius Barbeau rejected the collection,
accusing Street of having 'taken some slight material and
"written it up" – romanticized it.' In a letter to someone she
hoped might champion the manuscript, she complained that
'Dr. Dilworth [director of CBC western region] says the stories are artificial, Emily Car is definitely not interested ...
[and] Dr. Barbeau practically tells me I made them up.' In
response to her critics she privately confessed that two stories
– 'Croon Maiden' and 'Salmon Baby' – were not genuinely of
Sepass's 'Bible' stories. 'Croon Maiden' in particular she
admitted to having 'elaborated' upon, explaining that 'the
skeleton of the story is exact but it was so dramatic I did more
with it myself than the others,' and as a result she was 'quite
willing to take it out [of the collection] if that would be better.' Indeed, she admitted that Sepass himself had explained
to her that even his version of 'Croon Maiden' tale 'was not
one of the real ones.' Unable to persuade a publisher to assist
her, Street eventually self-published the collection (including
'Croon Maiden') in 1957 as *Sepass Poems*. A second version
appeared as *Sepass Tales*. See *Sepass Tales: The Songs of Y-ail-
Mihth*, 2nd ed. (Chilliwack, BC: Eloise Street, 1963); 3rd ed.
(Chilliwack, BC: Sepass Trust, 1974). See also Eloise Street to
William A. Newcomb, 14 October 1944, Add. Mss. 1077, Newcomb Family Papers, Correspondence, series A, vol. 12, folder
60, British Columbia Archives, Victoria, BC.

4 Originally 'Cat's Landing,' Katz Landing was a steamboat
   port adjacent to the Stó:lō community of Chawathil
   (Chowéthel) just west of Hope, BC. Elder Peter Dennis Peters
   explained that the name 'Katz Landing' originated when a
   pregnant cat walked off a gangplank as the steamboat was
   unloading cargo, and then upon the ship's return a few days
   later came back on board with her kittens.

5 In the 1860s the Catholic Oblate priests introduced a system
   of church-directed governance among the Stó:lō people

known as the Temperance Society. Society members swore off alcohol, and 'watchmen' were appointed by the priests to monitor people's behaviour and to report transgressions back to the church. In the following years, in response to challenges from Protestant missionaries and traditional hereditary leaders, the priests also appointed 'church chiefs,' many of whom were eventually recognized by the Canadian federal government as official representatives of the settlements.

6 Baptist Pat Charlie, son of Captain Charlie of Chawathil.

7 Webster lived on Whleach Island.

8 The Stó:lõ community just east of Aggasiz in the central Fraser Valley. Originally set aside in 1879 as a commonage reserve to meet the agricultural land needs of the residents of the seven upriver Stó:lõ bands, it became an independent band with its own Chief and council in 1960.

9 Fr. Eugene-Casimir Chirouse, OMI (not to be confused with his prominent missionary uncle of the same name), was a close advisor of Bishop Paul Durieu, and closely associated with promoting and overseeing the quasi-judicial Indian Temperance Societies of the late nineteenth and early twentieth centuries. He is infamous for being charged in civil court in 1892 for approving the severe whipping of a young Lillooet girl found guilty by the Temperance Society elders of sexual misconduct. After this disgrace, Chirouse the younger played a central role in organizing the impressive Indian 'Passion plays' that captured the imagination of non-Native imaginations in the years prior to the First World War.

10 The Canadian National Railroad was completed in 1913.

Works Cited

Bancroft, Hubert Howe. *History of British Columbia, 1792–1887*. San Francisco: History, 1887.

Boas, Franz. 'Indian Tribes of the Lower Fraser River.' In *64th Report of the British Association for the Advancement of Science for 1890*. London, 1894.

Brumble, David. *Annotated Bibliography of American Indian and Eskimo Bibliographies*. Lincoln: University of Nebraska Press, 1981.

– *American Indian Autobiography*. Berkeley: University of California Press, 1988.

Campbell, Maria. *Halfbreed*. Toronto: McClelland and Stewart, 1973.

Carlson, Keith, with Sonny McHalsie. *'I Am Stó:lõ!': Katherine Explores Her Heritage*. Chilliwack, BC: Stó:lõ Heritage Trust, 1998.

Carlson, K.T. 'Reflections on Indigenous History and Memory: Reconstructing and Reconsidering Contact.' In *Contact*, ed. John Lutz. Vancouver: UBC Press, forthcoming.

Culleton, Beatrice. *In Search of April Raintree*. Winnipeg: Pemmican, 1983.

Deloria, Vine. *Custer Died for Your Sins: An Indian Manifesto*. New York: Macmillan, 1969.

Dion, J. *My Tribe the Crees*. Calgary: Glenbow Museum, 1979.

Gates, Henry Louis. *The Signifying Monkey: A Theory of African-*

American Literary Criticism. London: Oxford University Press, 1989.

Glavin, Terry. *Amongst God's Own: The Enduring Legacy of St Mary's Mission*. Mission, BC: Longhouse, 2002.

Haig-Brown, Celia. *Resistance and Renewal: Surviving the Indian Residential School*. Vancouver: Tillacum Library, 1988.

Hancock, Robert L.A. 'The Hop Yards: Work Place and Social Place.' In *A Stó:lō Coast Salish Historical Atlas*, ed. Keith Thor Carlson, 70–1. Vancouver: Douglas & McIntyre, 2000.

Hauka, Donald. *McGowan's War*. Vancouver: New Star Books, 2003.

Hawthorn, H.B., ed. *Economic, Political, Educational Needs and Policies*. Vol. 2 of *A Survey of the Contemporary Indians of Canada*. *Ottawa*: Indian Affairs Branch, 1967.

Hilbert, V. 'Poking Fun in Looshootseed.' In *Working Papers for the 18th International Conference on Salish and Neighboring Languages*. Seattle: University of Washington Press, 1983.

Holden, M. 'Making All the Crooked Ways Straight: The Satirical Portrait of Whites in Coastal Salish Folklore.' *Journal of American Folklore* 89 (1976): 271–93.

Hoy, Helen. '"And use the words that were hers": Beverly Hungry Wolf's *The Ways of My Grandmothers*.' In *How Should I Read These? Native Women Writers in Canada*, 105–26. Toronto: University of Toronto Press, 2001.

– '"Nothing but the truth": Beatrice Culleton's *In Search of April Raintree*.' In *How Should I Read These? Native Women Writers in Canada*, 81–104. Toronto: University of Toronto Press, 2001.

King, Thomas. *The Truth about Stories: A Native Narrative*. Toronto: Anansi, 2003.

Knight, R. *Indians at Work: An Informal History of Native Labour in British Columbia, 1848–1930*. Vancouver: New Star Books, 1996.

Krech, Shepard, III. *The Ecological Indian: Myth and History*. New York: W.W. Norton, 1999.

Lawrence, S. Review of *Chiefly Indian*. *Raincoast Chronicles*, Book 3, 1972, 125.

Mackie, Richard Somerset. *Island Timber: A Social History of the Comox Logging Company, Vancouver Island.* Victoria: Sono Nis Press, 2000.

Maracle, Lee. *Bobbi Lee, Indian Rebel: Struggles of a Native Canadian Woman.* Richmond, BC: LSM Information Centre, 1975.

McIvor, Dorothy Matheson. *Coqualeetza: 'Vestiga nulla restrorsum.'* Williams Lake, BC: Blue Door Publishing, 2001.

Miller, J.R. *Shingwauk's Vision: A History of Native Residential Schools.* Toronto: University of Toronto Press, 1996.

Moore, James, 'The Discovery of Gold on Hill's Bar in 1858,' *BC Historical Quarterly* 3, no. 3 (1939): 215–20.

Nash, Roderick. *Wilderness and the American Mind.* 4th ed. New Haven: Yale University Press, 1999.

Nowell, C. *Smoke from Their Fires: The Life of a Kwakiutl Chief.* New Haven: Yale University Press, 1941.

Oelschlaeger, Max. *The Idea of Wilderness: From Prehistory to the Age of Ecology.* New Haven: Yale University Press, 1991.

Pennier, Henry. *Chiefly Indian: The Warm and Witty Story of a British Columbia Half Breed Logger.* Ed. Herbert L. McDonald. Vancouver: GrayDonald Graphics, 1972.

Raibmon, Paige. '"A New Understanding of Things Indian": George Raley's Negotiation of the Residential School Experience.' *BC Studies* 110 (Summer 1996): 69–96.

Sarris, Greg. *Keeping Slug Woman Alive: A Holistic Approach to American Indian Texts.* Berkeley: University of California Press, 1993.

Sewid, J. *Guests Never Leave Hungry: The Autobiography of James Sewid, a Kwakiutl Indian.* Montreal and Kingston: McGill-Queen's University Press, 1989.

Stalo Nation News. May 1978. Biography of Hank Pennier.

Swann, Brian, and Arnold Krupat, eds. *I Tell You Now: Autobiographical Essays by Native American Writers.* Lincoln: University of Nebraska Press, 1987.

Twigg, Alan. *Aboriginality: The Literary Origins of British Columbia.* Volume 2. Vancouver: Ronsdale, 2005.

Wapiti, M. *Ashes of the Fire: Manuscript of Just a Little Halfbreed.* Smithers, BC: Tanglewood, 1972.

Illustration Credits